To Begin Again

To Begin Again

REBUILDING YOUR LIFE
AFTER BAD THINGS HAVE
HAPPENED

Naomi Levy

Thorsons
An Imprint of HarperCollins*Publishers*

Thorsons
An Imprint of HarperCollins*Publishers*
77–85 Fulham Palace Road,
Hammersmith, London w6 8jb

First published in hardback by Alfred A. Knopf, Inc. 1998
This edition published by Thorsons 1999

1 3 5 7 9 10 8 6 4 2

© Naomi Levy 1998

Naomi Levy asserts her moral right to be
identified as the author of this work.

Grateful acknowledgement is made to the following
for permission to reprint previously published material:
The Jewish Publication Society: Prayer for Rabbi Nahman of Bratslav,
translated by Rabbi Shamai Kanter, from *The Third Jewish Catalog:
Creating Community*, compiled and edited by Sharon Strassfeld and Michael
Strassfeld, copyright © 1980 by Sharon Strassfeld and Michael Strassfeld.
Excerpts from "Isaish", "Jeremiah", "Job" and "The Song of Songs"
from *Tanakh: The Holy Scriptures*, copyright © 1985 by the
Jewish Publication Society. Reprinted by permission of the Jewish
Publication Society.
The Rabbinical Assembly: Excerpts from
"Psalm 116" from *Siddur Sim Shalom* (p. 385), edited by Rabbi
Jules Harlow, copyright © 1985 by The Rabbinical Assembly.

A catalogue record for this book
is available from the British Library

ISBN 0 7225 3819 7

Printed and bound in Great Britain by
Creative Print and Design (Wales), Ebbw Vale

For My Parents

George Levy, of blessed memory, and Ruth Levy

CONTENTS

Contents

ACKNOWLEDGMENTS

THIS BOOK EMERGED largely as a result of my seven years of service to Temple Mishkon Tephilo. Although I have stepped down from the pulpit, my congregants were and continue to be sources of inspiration and strength to me. I offer my deep respect and gratitude to Beth Cohen, Shari Davis and Michael Dubin, Ed Geil, Dennis and Kathy Gura, Goldie Shore, Sam and Eva Widawski, David and Dorothy and Jane, and Louis and Dina, and to all those whose heroic struggles appear in the book under assumed names. I thank them for sharing their lives with me so freely and for allowing me to tell their stories so they might be sources of healing to others. The memories of Lloyd Ehrenberg, Rebecca Gura, and Max Polsky are a blessing to all those whose lives they touched. I pray that I have done justice to the precious lessons they have taught me.

My agent, Esther Newberg, supported this endeavor from the time of our very first phone call and has been an indispensable adviser and advocate ever since. Peter Gethers, my editor at Knopf, shepherded this book from start to finish. He provided his superb editorial skills, his unwavering faith in this work, and his much-welcome reassurance and guidance. Many thanks to Pat Johnson for her patience and understanding; to Melvin Rosenthal for his precision; to Esther's assistant, Jack Horner; to Peter's associate Amy Scheibe and his assistant Newley Purnell, who kept things running smoothly; and to Elise Solomon for her legal counsel.

Acknowledgments

My friend Ed Solomon made it possible for me to seek out the best agent and publisher. He pored over this manuscript, pushed me to be as honest as I could, and offered me his sound advice.

William Goldman has become my writing rabbi. He guided me patiently, showed me how to work through periods of writer's block, and taught me to believe that my words could help others in pain.

Daniel Adler believed in this work from the start. He read my manuscript with intense attention and offered his unique assistance. Many thanks to Jessie Nelson for her honesty and deep understanding. And to Brett Barenholtz, Jack Behr, Chana and Phil Bell, Cynthia Cleese, Ron Eldard and Julianna Margulies, Carole Eule, Susan Goland and Russell Schwartz, Edzia Goldstein, Brian Gordon, Dr. Jeff Gornbein, Lori Grafstein, Stig Jantz, Jane Kagon and Ed Greenberg, Murray Kalis, Andrea and Warren Kay, Callie Khouri and David Warfield, Jonathan Kirsch, Avery and Betsy Krut, Donna Malamud and Tom Laichas, Leonard Nelson, Rebecca Ritter, Dani Rosen and Jim Morton, Dr. Helene Rosenzweig, Carin Sage, Dr. Dawne Schoenholz, Teresa Strasser, Lazare Tannenbaum, Carol Taubman, Ella Taylor, Shifra Teitelbaum, Rabbi Stewart Vogel, Gary Wexler, Marvin Wolf, Rabbi David Wolpe, and Dianne Arieff Zaga, who all freely gave of their time and insight. To Sophie, who made it all possible. And to all the others who are too numerous to name who heard me out and brainstormed with me. To Daniel Brookman for his generous legal assistance. And many thanks to Dr. Frank Kwong and Lorena Munoz.

Rabbi Burton L. Visotzky has been a source of sage counsel. He read this work and painstakingly reviewed all the specifically religious references. Of course, any errors are my responsibility alone. Father Edward Berumen read my words with the depth and sensitivity he applies to all his endeavors. Rabbi Elliot Dorff, Dr. Richard Polenberg, and Dr. David Roskies all read this manuscript, offered me their insight, and reminded me to choose my words wisely.

Today is my father's yahrzeit, the anniversary of his death. It has been twenty years since I last saw him and I miss him every single day. But not even death can obliterate his presence in my life, which continues to fill me with strength, courage, and passion.

My mother has journeyed from darkness to life and has taught me that the human spirit is truly invincible. She has allowed me to write about her struggles in this book and is forever available to offer me her wisdom, encouragement, and love.

My sister, Dr. Miriam Levy, and brothers Dr. Daniel Levy and David Levy have all heroically found the courage to return to life and joy. They are role models of strength to me and are always available to talk and help whenever times get difficult. My mother and siblings read my words with the greatest of care and offered me their sound and loving advice.

My in-laws, Sari and Aaron Eshman, have given me constant reassurance and support. They have also always been there to assist in any way possible so that I might sneak away and write.

My sisters- and brothers-in-law, nieces and nephews, aunts, uncles, and cousins, have all been sources of encouragement and joy. I remember my departed relatives with gratitude and love.

My husband, Robert Eshman, is a rare soul. Our life together is a gift from God. My respect, admiration, and love for him are deeper than I can possibly describe in words. His influence on this book is everywhere. He has given me his ear, his criticism, this book's title, his advice, his keen editorial eye,

Acknowledgments

his constant encouragement, his wisdom, his mouth-watering meals, his patience in reading this manuscript, more times than he would care to remember, and his love.

My son, Adin Joseph, and my daughter, Noa Rakia, are my greatest blessings, my inspiration, my light, and my comfort.

Whole and complete, this work is my prayer to God, Creator of all.

18 Sivan 5758
June 1998
Venice, California

PART ONE

Pain and Its Aftermath

Every one of us has suffered a hurt that has robbed us of something much larger than the actual hurt itself. Just as a solitary pebble can cause an entire pond to ripple, a single painful experience can have far-reaching effects on our lives.

CHAPTER ONE

Resurrection

"PUSH!" I cried. "Push! Push! Push!"

Michelle held her breath and her face turned deep red. The baby's heartbeat was slowing. A nurse shoved me aside and fastened an oxygen mask around Michelle's face. "Push!" I insisted.

"Who's *she*?" the nurse asked, looking in my direction. "She's our rabbi," Michelle's husband Paul responded. The nurse thought he was kidding and laughed.

The doctor raced in and, without explaining why, ordered the nurses to quickly roll Michelle's bed from the birthing room to the operating room. Paul and I threw on sterile blue gowns, masks, and caps. I kept cheering "Push!" over and over again. My heart was racing. Something in the doctor's expression made me worry. Was the baby in danger? Was *Michelle* in danger? The fetal monitor beeped, the IV bag dripped, and the blood pressure cuff hissed, but to my absolute amazement, not a sound escaped from Michelle's lips. During the breaks between contractions, I recited prayers for a safe delivery and the health of the baby. Paul held his wife's hand, his grip conveying a loving calm.

One more push, then a miracle: the baby's head began to crown.

A few more minutes of excruciating pain, which Michelle endured in silence, and the baby pressed its way through the birth canal. Soon the raspy cry of a beautiful baby boy filled the air. A new life breath, a sweet fragile soul entered this universe.

As she held her child swaddled and safe, Michelle looked up at me. "I almost lost my life," she whispered. "I know," I responded. But neither one of us was thinking about the danger she had just come through. We were remembering another time.

IT WAS the day after Yom Kippur and I was emotionally and physically drained. It had been a grueling two months of preparation for the High Holy Days, but now they were over. I was relaxing in my study, still reeling from the previous evening. The service had been the most moving of my life. I had never felt such holiness in the sanctuary. The entire congregation had fused into a single voice of prayer. As I was reflecting on the experience, my intercom beeped. "There's someone here to see you, Rabbi," my assistant said.

I walked to the front door of the synagogue, still in a reverential daze, and there stood a woman with two black eyes hidden behind her dark sunglasses, a broken nose, bruises everywhere. I held Michelle's arm and led her to my study. She could barely walk. I was mortified. I had seen her just the week before at Sabbath services. Now, as she sat in my study, I could hardly believe this was the same person. Not knowing how to begin, I waited for her to speak, but she refused to look my way. She stared at the floor, and when she finally raised her face, she looked out beyond me as if I weren't there sitting before her.

She broke the silence with one word: "Why?"

I waited for more. And slowly she began to speak.

On the afternoon before Yom Kippur, Michelle had showered and dressed in her holiday clothes. She was on her way to a festive meal with her best friend. Afterward the two of them were going to come to synagogue to begin the daylong fast. She picked up her keys, locked the door to her apartment, and walked toward her car. Suddenly a man came up from behind and grabbed her. When she resisted, he punched her in the face, knocked her to the floor, and beat her. Then he picked Michelle up, opened the trunk of her car, threw her in, and slammed it shut. The engine started to roar, and soon the car was moving. It was pitch-black in that trunk and Michelle was terrified. Her entire body shook in fear. Where was he taking her? Was he planning to kill her? Would he dispose of her body in a place where she would never be found? All she could do in the blinding darkness was say to herself over and over again, "I want to live! I want to live!" The car stopped. The trunk opened, her eyes were assaulted by the stinging sunlight. He dragged her into the backseat. He raped her. And then he let her go.

When she finished speaking, Michelle remained silent for a long while. Then, from behind the dark sunglasses, she looked at me for the first time and quietly asked, "Where was God? Was God so busy at the Yom Kippur service in synagogue that God forgot about me?"

I kept silent. I didn't want to offer her any platitudes. Searching my mind for answers, I found that I had none to offer. All I had were questions. Just the night before, at the concluding service of Yom Kippur, I had felt so complete, so whole in my faith. In the sanctuary that night, all of us who were there had chanted, "O Lord our God, have mercy upon us, watch over us, grant us a good life in the coming year." Yom Kippur had ended with such words of hope. I had left the synagogue and returned home filled with the conviction that it was going to be a good year. A year of strength and health. But as I sat beside Michelle the very next morning, all I could think to myself was, "Why did this happen? How could God have *let* it happen?"

We both sat in silence for a long time, then Michelle said, "Yesterday was also my birthday." What a strange and horrible coincidence. I said to her quietly, "And you lived to see it." She replied, "But I'm not sure I want to be alive. I don't know if I can carry on."

Michelle was overwhelmed by so many horrible feelings. She felt betrayed and abandoned, violated and petrified, angry and dirty and ashamed and alone. She was silent again for a long while. Then she asked, "Can we pray the Kol Nidre?"

Yom Kippur was over, and the time for praying the Kol Nidre, the opening service of Yom Kippur, had passed. According to Jewish law, there is a very precise time when the Kol Nidre may be said. The service must take place before sunset on the eve of Yom Kippur. On the other hand, as Tevye the milkman loved to say, there is always an other hand. In this case, I believed that God would accept the prayer regardless of its late date.

I stood up, took Michelle's hand, and helped her to her feet. We walked slowly into the pitch-black sanctuary. I turned on the lights and pulled out two prayer books. Then I opened the Holy Ark, carefully removed a Torah scroll, and placed it in her arms. She grasped it like a child clutching her mother. We stood side by side on the pulpit, the two of us alone in the large empty space. She swayed gently with the Torah in her arms, while I chanted the words of the Kol Nidre. We were both trembling, and as we stood there, an eerie feeling came over me. Usually the Kol Nidre is a service of repentance. It is a time when we beat our breasts and ask God to pardon us for all our sins. But in the sanctuary that day after Yom Kippur, I could have sworn that it was not Michelle who was repenting. It was God. It was God, I imagined, who was beating a breast, who was praying to *Michelle* for forgiveness.

By the second repetition of the prayer, I could see a calm settle in Michelle's face. At the third repetition, the tears came pouring out of both of us. And when we could cry no more, we returned the Torah to the ark.

When we got back to my study, I wondered to myself

whether there was something more I could do. Was there anything I could say to take away her pain? Were there any words to describe how much I wanted to help? Then she said to me, "I always thought that God was my protector. I guess I was wrong." I told Michelle I didn't believe that God had forgotten her. I said that I firmly believed God was with her, even inside that dark trunk. I said, "If God could prevent all tragedies from occurring, then there would *be* no tragedies. I don't believe that's in God's hands." She said, "Then what good is God?"

The question stopped me short.

Being a rabbi means I am asked questions every day of my life. Some questions are easy: What time do we light Sabbath candles this week? Or, how many Jews make up a prayer quorum? But most of the important ones are unanswerable. I used to have a running joke with Sam, the sexton at my synagogue. Every time a question arose, he knew how I was going to respond. He'd ask, "Rabbi, what should we do about such and such?" And I'd say, "Sam, what do you think?" Then he would start to laugh. He'd say, "A rabbi is supposed to have all the answers." "Sam," I would reply, "a rabbi is supposed to have all the *questions.*"

People have asked me so many impossible questions. Is God punishing me for my sins by striking my child with this illness? Should I keep the baby or should I have an abortion? Should I leave my wife? Should I divorce my husband? Does prayer have healing powers? Can it cure my cancer? Should I tell my wife about an affair I had, or would it be better to keep it to myself? Do I have to forgive my father for abusing me? Is there any way to repent for having killed two people while driving under the influence?

But by far the most difficult question I've ever faced was the one posed by Michelle: "What good is God?"

Dozens of responses raced through my mind. Then I thought about my own life and my own struggles with God. I realized that this was not the time to defend or explain God. This was a time to offer comfort. We hugged long and hard, then said goodbye. And I thought: There are questions that can never be answered properly with words. The answers are not matters of logic. Nor are they about philosophy or theology. Each one of us carries a question for which there is no answer. Why is this world filled with such ugliness and cruelty? Why did my loved one have to die? Why must I suffer? What are we to do with these painful questions? Where should we be searching for answers? Will we ever find them?

Many people assume that because I am a rabbi I spend my days trying to explain why God created a world that is so full of tragedies. I don't. I can't. Nor have I ever heard from any religious leader an answer to that question that has satisfied me. The question I have tried to answer again and again, both for my own life and for the lives of my congregants who have come to me in pain, is not: Why did this happen? But: How will I go on?

IT HAS BEEN a little over seven years now since that terrible crime was committed against Michelle. And it has been a very difficult and painful time for her. A time of fear and depression, of anger and shame and struggles. She stopped working. She moved out of her apartment. Worried that she had perhaps brought this attack upon herself, for a long while she could not bring herself to wear anything even vaguely feminine. She was haunted by flashbacks. For many months she lived with the fear that she had been infected with the deadly AIDS virus. Scared to drive anywhere alone, she stayed home by herself much of the time. Every birthday brought with it a renewed dose of depression and fearsome flashbacks. Every Yom Kippur was a nightmare to be relived.

But somehow Michelle found a path back to life. Somehow

she found the way to trust again. Eventually, she allowed a man to get close to her. She fell in love with him and they married. As I stood before her and Paul under the wedding canopy, performing their marriage ceremony, I thought to myself, "Resurrection is possible." When, after a number of years of waiting and trying, Michelle took me aside one Sabbath and whispered, "I'm pregnant," I thought to myself, "Resurrection is indeed possible." And when that blessed baby came forth from her holy body, I uttered the ancient blessing, "Blessed is the One who gives life to the dead."

But how did this resurrection occur? What enabled Michelle to overcome her pain and fears? To open herself up to love? To trust again? To want to bring a fragile child into this all-too-uncertain world? To forgive God?

Five years after her rape, Michelle sat on that same chair in my study with her tiny son suckling at her breast. Once again we walked together into the sanctuary, and we stood on the same pulpit where we had stood that awful day. But this time the room was filled with onlookers, rejoicing as her son was placed on the table for his bris, his ritual circumcision. And as he was brought into the covenant of our people, the community cheered "Mazel tov!" I stood on the pulpit beside Michelle with tears in my eyes, singing and clapping.

To FIND OUR WAY back to hope and joy, as Michelle did, is perhaps the hardest task each of us can face. Whatever our hardships have been, so many of us find ourselves merely surviving, just going through the motions. Many of us have long since given up the struggle. Perhaps we have lived through hell. Or feel trapped or alone. Perhaps we have been hurt, betrayed, abandoned. Or have suffered losses, illness. Perhaps we have grown callous and bitter. Perhaps we have forgotten a very simple yet crucial truth: Each of us possesses the power to overcome the unthinkable and be reborn, to live life not as survivors but as partakers, rejoicers, participants.

But what *is* the path back to life? Why are some people unable to embark on that journey? What makes others so capable of rebirth? We all know someone who has been permanently crippled by a hurt, someone who has become cynical and untrusting, fearful and unable to move forward. I have been in that position. My guess is, so has almost anyone reading this book. But we also know someone who has astounded us by responding to pain with a rare combination of resiliency and hope. How is that possible? What are the steps that restore people to life and to faith?

This is a question I have asked myself over and over again. During my years in the pulpit I also posed it to my congregants. They shared with me their pain and their courage, their strength and their faith, their wisdom and their insights.

WHEN I WAS in rabbinical school, I never planned on leading my own congregation. After leaving the seminary, I was working happily in a university when a member of Temple Mishkon Tephilo's board of directors phoned me. He told me about his congregation in Venice, California, then asked if I might be interested in applying for their rabbinic position. I responded with a definitive no. I wasn't sure that synagogues were ready to embrace women rabbis, and I was in no hurry to pioneer that cause. I also had terrible stage fright. The idea of speaking before a congregation petrified me. But this man was persistent. He kept calling and calling. Finally, I agreed to come and have a look. Still, I was so ambivalent about this meeting that I waited until the last possible second to buy proper interview clothes. I raced to a clothing store and told the salesperson that I had a job interview that night, but the only suit she had to offer me was a size too large. So she took me aside and said, "Listen to me, darling, wear it with the tags tonight, bring it back tomorrow, and I'll order you the right size." I grabbed the suit and sped off.

That night I walked up the steps to the temple and shook hands with the members of the search committee; then we sat down to talk. They fired questions at me—about my background, my beliefs, my interests, my Judaic knowledge. They posed hypothetical scenarios and asked how I would respond in each case. An older man asked me to explain how I, as a young woman, would be able to offer advice to people who were old enough to be my grandparents. The whole time we spoke, I kept praying that the price tag wouldn't suddenly pop out from under my sleeve. We met for over two hours; then I asked to see the sanctuary.

The moment I set foot inside, I knew in the depths of my being that I had come home. A chill shot up my spine. The path before me suddenly seemed so clear and so certain I knew instantly that I had entered the next leg of my journey through life.

Mishkon Tephilo, meaning "home of prayer," is a congregation of some two hundred families. My congregants were mostly under forty or over seventy. Membership had been declining for years, until a lot of younger people moved into the neighborhood and began to get involved. The building is a stately but simple structure situated just a block from the Pacific Ocean, sandwiched between trendy boutiques, gyms, cafés, and a New Age bookstore, and just across from Arnold Schwarzenegger's office. The stores turn over year after year, but the synagogue remains the one constant in this city of fads and fashions.

In my first days there, I felt like such a kid and worried that my congregants would never take me seriously as their rabbi. But a wise colleague of mine explained: "Naomi, when you start marrying them and burying them, you will become their rabbi." And he was perfectly right. Initially, people *did* treat me like a curiosity. But it wasn't long before I went from being their new young woman rabbi to being their rabbi. Even my stage fright melted away, and over time I began to find my true voice.

As I settled into my position as rabbi of Mishkon Tephilo, I quickly realized that nothing could have prepared me for the life that was unfolding before me—not for the intensity of joy I would experience, not for the depths of pain I would also come to experience.

I fell in love with the temple and with my job almost immediately. The people were so warm, and so eager to learn. The thing I liked most about my synagogue was that it was thoroughly unpretentious. At my services, people came dressed casually, some even in shorts and jeans; children pranced up and down the aisles. The focus was always on faith, not on appearances. I quickly shed my business suits for casual clothes and got to work. I soon abandoned the more formal speaking style I had studied in rabbinical school and began to speak from my heart.

My responsibilities ranged from the holy to the mundane. I tutored bar and bat mitzvah students, prepared my sermons, and taught adult education classes at night. To see people so eager to study after they had just come from a long and busy day at work was a source of constant inspiration to me. Every day people came to me with their questions, their problems, their moral dilemmas, their rage, their stories. I offered them my ear, my heart, my counsel. I'm sure that when they came to me for advice they never realized how much they were helping and teaching me about faith and about God. Presiding over baby-namings, circumcisions, bar and bat mitzvahs, weddings, and funerals also taught me much about the never-ending cycle of life. The joyous occasions always reminded me how miraculous life is. The tragedies always forced me to remember how fragile our lives are, and how fleeting. Sometimes I would have to perform a wedding and a funeral back-to-back. I saw firsthand how joy can turn to pain, and how pain can also give way to joy. My most powerful spiritual experiences took place when I would lead my community in prayer each Friday night and Saturday morning. Occasionally we would take our prayers to the beach, and the fervor that came forth from hundreds of us singing, dancing, and praying to God on the sand, before the ocean, beneath the vast expanse of the sky, was truly breathtaking. And then, of course, there were the routine responsibilities—the numerous committee meetings, the never-ending administrative tasks, the fund-raising duties—that were also integral aspects of my pulpit life.

After seven years at the synagogue, and many months of soul-searching, I decided to step down from my pulpit. It was a decision made with more than a little ambivalence and with much trepidation. I left in order to spend more time with my two small children—my most precious and important responsibilities. But I continue to pray together with the members of this remarkable community, and I continue to reflect on the lessons they have taught me.

In the pages that follow, what you will find are stories. My story and the stories of my congregants, intertwined with the wisdom and lessons of my religion and faith, Judaism. I believe that these stories go a long way toward answering the questions we all need answered no matter what pains we have suffered. I believe they can help us make the journey from tragedy and grief back to life.

Throughout the book I have also included prayers I've composed that give me strength to carry on. I hope they are helpful, but please use them only as preludes—don't let them be obstacles—to your own unique way of relating to God or to your own source of strength.

Sometimes when we're suffering we feel as if we have been singled out. We wonder why God has picked on us. But my life as the rabbi of a small synagogue taught me that if that's what we think, we are mistaken. We are never alone in our suffering.

Scratch the surface of any family, any social gathering, any congregation, and you will find loss and pain there. We may not always be privy to the pain, but it is there just the same. If we had the power to peer inside the heart of any human being, we would uncover there a silent anguish. I didn't need to look any further than my own little temple for heroic tales of suffering and triumph. In fact, I couldn't even begin to fit all the moving experiences in my community into this one book.

I hope the lessons I have learned from my congregation can be a source of inspiration and comfort to people of all faiths. Words that come from the heart enter the heart, an ancient rabbinic proverb instructs us. The words in this book come from the heart—mine and the hearts of others. I pray that you will find within them a spark that will ignite the flame of hope and the passion for healing that lies within us all.

A PRAYER

Teach me always to believe in my power to return to life, to hope, and to You, my God, no matter what pains I have endured, no matter how far I have strayed from You. Give me the strength to resurrect my weary spirit. Revive me, God, and I will embrace life once more in joy, in passion, in peace.
Amen.

CHAPTER TWO

Tragedy and Its Impact

A FEW YEARS AGO a man named Jim came to see me. He was over six feet tall with a thick head of light-blond hair and a ruddy complexion. He sat in my study and said, "This is the first time I've been in a synagogue in over twenty-seven years." I said, "I'm glad you've come. Why have you stayed away so long?" He fidgeted, his eyes welled up with tears, and out came his story: "My father died when I was a young boy. My mother didn't really know what to do with me, so she used to send me to the synagogue. I loved it. I think the old men there took pity on me. They adopted me, and the synagogue became like a second father to me. After my bar mitzvah the rabbi was so taken with me that he asked me to read from the Torah in front of the whole congregation on Yom Kippur. Of course, I said I'd love to. I felt so important and so honored. During those weeks, as I was practicing my Torah portion, all the sadness of my home life seemed to fade into the background. The night before Yom Kippur, I was so excited I couldn't sleep. In the morning I jumped out of bed, got dressed in my bar mitzvah suit, the only suit I owned, and ran to the synagogue. When I got to the entrance, an usher was standing at the door, and he said to me, 'Where's your ticket?' I looked up at him and said proudly, 'I don't have a ticket. I'm reading from the Torah today.' But the usher said, 'I don't care what you think you're reading. You're not getting in without a ticket.'" Choking back tears, Jim continued his story. He said, "I turned around and ran home crying. I suppose that I've never stopped running." He wiped away his tears and continued, "I know that the usher was just one stupid person trying to do his job, but somehow in my mind he came to represent all of Judaism. I thought to myself, if all this religion cares about is who has a ticket and who doesn't, then I don't want anything to do with it."

I asked Jim if he had ever spoken to his rabbi about this. He said he hadn't. "Don't you think he might have been able to set things straight?" I asked. He said, "I don't know. I was so hurt that I just left."

I told Jim how glad I was that he had shared this hurt with me. I said I hoped he would come back to synagogue more often, to see that his religion is a caring one, and that his synagogue is filled mostly with good and kind people.

As he was leaving, I thought to myself how sad it is that the actions of one insensitive person can have such a devastating effect on our lives. It doesn't seem fair that one misguided human being was able to rob a young, fatherless child of the comfort of his religion—not just for one day, or one year, but for twenty-seven years. What about all of those loving old men who had doted on this boy in the synagogue? Why didn't their kindness and love outweigh the cruelty of the usher in this boy's mind?

Every one of us who has suffered pain knows that the blow itself is always accompanied by fallout. A bomb can hit its target head-on, but the damage from the blast may destroy everything surrounding the target as well. A divorce can cause us to fear intimacy. A failure in business can destroy our confidence. An illness can cause us to feel isolated and alone.

A death can shatter our world.

. . .

EACH DAY when my father came home from work, my mother would run into his arms. The two of them would stand motionless by the front door in a desperate embrace like lovers reunited at an airport. They stood at the exact same height—both five foot three. They called each other "Doodles." I never heard them call each other by their first names.

My parents always seemed to be in each other's arms. Neither I nor any of my three older siblings can ever remember them fighting. Quite the opposite—they were always singing. In my family, singing was the way we related to one another. Sometimes we'd sit down to lunch on the Sabbath and just harmonize for hours. On Passover we would gather around the seder table and sing every Passover melody we knew until two or three in the morning. Every Simchat Torah, the holiday when Jews celebrate the conclusion of the year's Torah reading cycle, my parents held an open house.

We had a small home occupying the first floor of a three-family house in Brooklyn. My sister Mimi and I were eleven and a half years apart, but we shared a bedroom. I was playing with dolls when she was already dating. There was quite an age difference between me and my siblings. I was born when my mother was forty. Once I asked her if I was an accident. She smiled and said, "Let's just say you were a pleasant surprise."

My two older brothers, David and Danny, were a most unlikely match, but they too were roommates. David was a total mess, while Danny was meticulously neat. David's idea of cleaning up was to shove everything from old candy wrappers to dirty T-shirts under his bed. Danny ironed his own clothing. David had a voracious appetite; after a meal he'd finish off the leftovers on everybody's plate. Danny was slight. The six of us shared one bathroom and one telephone. Waiting for a turn at the bathroom—and waiting and waiting and waiting—was a way of life. We had no dining room and only a tiny kitchen. So at Simchat Torah, in order to make room for all our guests, we would move our beds down to the basement. Weeks in advance, my mother baked dozens of cakes and stored them in the freezers of aunts and friends. When the holiday arrived, over one hundred people gathered in our home to sing and dance and feast. Dozens of people would walk in right off the street and join us. I can still picture my father sitting in the living room surrounded by all his friends: Saul Gladstone, Hy Saposh, Moishe Rubinstein, Sam Sloan. I can still hear his voice belting out song after song.

When my father was singing or praying or studying, he was remarkably outgoing. But when it came to ordinary conversation, he was peculiarly silent. In fact, he had no idea how to make even the simplest small talk. If he had something specific to say, he said it. Otherwise he was either silent or singing. My father and I connected through study and song.

One day, when I was fifteen, my father came home early from work and asked if I'd like to go to the aquarium with him. I was shocked. In my entire life my father had never taken me to a single secular activity. My older sister and two brothers had known my father before he became so deeply passionate about Judaism. They had known him before he injured his hip. They remember the days when our kitchen wasn't kosher, and when my father used to drink the occasional beer. He injured his hip during a baseball game as he was sliding into second base, and I think that injury contributed to his religious awakening. He could no longer participate in sports, every step he took was painful, so he began to find ways of living through his mind and heart. My paternal grandmother's death also played a crucial role. He began going to synagogue to recite the Kaddish, the mourner's prayer, for her, and there he discovered a religious fervor that had long been lying dormant inside him. As my sister and brothers began studying for their bat and bar mitzvahs, my father started to study together with them. Perhaps my

Pain and Its Aftermath

father's age made him more susceptible to religious feelings, as did his unfulfilling work—the daily grind at the clothing factory which brought him little financial reward and even less satisfaction. In his forties he was a prime candidate for a midlife crisis. Judaism offered him a path to deep joy and eternal meaning.

The very idea of my father ever playing baseball is unfathomable to me. The father I knew lived in constant physical pain, walked with a limp, and went to synagogue for leisure. So you can imagine how taken aback I was by his invitation to visit the aquarium with him. Of course I accepted. We drove all the way to Coney Island in perfect silence. Sometimes the silence felt painful because it was so intense; I wished there were a way to lighten it up with idle chatter. But most of the time it felt comforting, as if we didn't need to say anything when we were together.

When we got to the aquarium, we walked around hand in hand. My father told me that his favorite animals were the penguins. We stood there watching those penguins for close to twenty minutes, hardly saying a word to each other, just holding hands. It felt so good simply to be with him.

That night, I was lying on my parents' bed watching television when my father came in, sat down, and said, "Nomi, I want to teach you a song." I sat up and he began to sing a beautiful Yiddish love song, "Papir Iz Doch Vays." First he translated it for me, then he sang each line over and over again until I picked up both the melody and the words. Then we sang it together.

> Just as paper is white, and ink is black,
> So does my heart long for you, my dearest.
> I could sit for days on end,
> Kissing your sweet face and holding your hand.

When my father was satisfied that I had mastered the song, he looked at me misty-eyed from behind his thick glasses and

19

said, "This was the last song my mother taught me before she died."

It was the last song my father ever taught me.

IT WAS a hot and muggy Tuesday, June 20, 1978. I was fifteen. I took the city bus to Yeshiva of Flatbush High School to find out my score on the State Regents exam in biology. I learned that I had gotten 98 percent! Exhilarated and relieved, I met up with my girlfriends Linda, Debbie, and Shifra, and together we went out to celebrate. We walked to the Kent movie theater at Avenue I and Coney Island Avenue to catch the 1:00 p.m. showing of *Saturday Night Fever*. Wearing a white T-shirt, a jeans skirt, blue argyle knee socks, and maroon clogs, I bopped down the street with my Dorothy Hamill haircut, cracking my chewing gum over and over again. When we arrived at the theater, the movie had already begun. From the lobby I could hear the Bee Gees singing: "Ah, ah, ah, ah, stayin' alive, stayin' alive." We found our seats in the dark, overly air-conditioned room. It was a welcome coolness. I shivered, curled myself up in a ball in my seat with my knees tucked under my chin, and lost myself in the film.

The movie was set in Brooklyn, but it was another Brooklyn from the one I knew. I lived in Boro Park, an exclusively Jewish, and mostly Hasidic, neighborhood. Though my family was not Orthodox, I attended a private Orthodox yeshiva high school. Bensonhurst, the neighborhood depicted in the film, was only two miles from my home, but I'd never been there. The disco culture, with its polyester clothes and thick Brooklyn accents, was as far from my world as the moon. The closest I had ever gotten to sex was a French kiss in summer camp. The closest I had ever gotten to crime was watching Ken Solomon steal a Snickers bar from the luncheonette across the street from my school.

When the movie was over, we all confessed to a crush on John Travolta, and we all agreed that we would never have sex in the backseat of a car, not even with John Travolta. Then we went our separate ways. I came home and shared the good news about my grades with my parents. They were thrilled. My mother, who was always worrying about my perfectionism, told me that I shouldn't pressure myself to top the grades I had gotten that semester. My father said, "Nonsense. Nomi, you can do better still!" After dinner I went out again with my friend Shifra. We walked to Baskin-Robbins to get some ice cream. The guy behind the counter flirted with me and I flirted back. He gave me a double scoop for the price of a single: vanilla fudge swirl and peppermint. Shifra and I walked home licking our cones, trying to keep up with the steady stream of ice cream dripping down our hands and forearms. As we walked, I imitated John Travolta's gait and sang, "Ah, ah, ah, ah, stayin' alive, stayin' alive."

When I got home again, like any healthy teenage girl, I closed the door to my room and called my boyfriend. I was busy gabbing on the phone when my mother walked in. She was having another of her acute asthma attacks and told me, "The doctor said he could see me tonight, so Daddy and I are going over there now. We'll see you later." I said "Bye" and continued my two-hour conversation. When I hung up the phone, I was so tired that I put my head down and fell asleep.

The next thing I remember, my mother and sister were shaking me awake. I was delirious from sleep, but somehow in my dream I thought I heard them say something. The words filtered through my sleep in a blur, and as I started to wake up, I thought they said, "The doctor gave Daddy a shot." I turned over and tucked my head beneath the covers. But still they kept shaking me: "Wake up, Nomi."

"So what?" I moaned in a cranky voice. "So what if he got a shot?"

I opened my eyes and they were both standing over me in tears. "Nomi, you've got to get dressed and come with us to the hospital. Daddy's been shot."

When I fully awoke, I learned what had happened. My mother and father were walking from the doctor's office to their car when a man came at them with a gun and tried to rob them. The attacker panicked, shot my father in the stomach, then ran away. My father was rushed to the hospital. At the very moment my mother and sister were waking me up, he was undergoing a long and grueling surgery. I was in shock, unable to believe the words they were saying. I jumped out of bed and got dressed, and the three of us raced back to the hospital.

Time stopped. The medicinal stench of the hospital was like a slap in the face that told me, "This is no dream." My sister, who was a medical student herself, kept repeating over and over again, "He's not going to make it. He's not going to make it." I wanted to silence her. "So what if she's a doctor," I thought. "Isn't there any room for hope? For a miracle?"

After seven hours in surgery, my father was placed in intensive care. That evening when we went in to see him, he was unconscious. His entire body was filling up with fluid. His face was so bloated that they couldn't fit his eyeglasses around his ears, no matter how far they tried to stretch them. There were wires and tubes coming out of all different parts of his body. There was a tube down his throat attached to a respirator that forced air into his lungs. In-out. In-out. In-out. The sound of that pump drove me to distraction. It seemed so cruel to force someone to breathe like that. We encircled his bed, and each one of us said something to him. These were my exact words: "Hi, Daddy. You look great. Get better soon."

Those were the last words I ever said to my father. I never saw him again. I hated those words after I spoke them. They seemed so forced, so foolish.

The next day the doctors noticed that my father kept flailing his arms about. They thought these were merely strange jerking responses and that he was still unconscious. But one of the nurses put a pen in my father's hand and gave him a pad of paper. He immediately started to write. Suddenly there was hope. My father was aware of everything around him. My mother went in, spoke to him, and got written responses back. So did my sister and brothers. They reported that he was as witty as ever, even cracking jokes. I waited anxiously for my turn to talk to him, but it never came. The doctors said that my father had had enough excitement for one day and that he needed to rest. I could come back tomorrow. But somehow, in my heart, I knew that my turn would never come.

The next morning my father was taken into surgery once more. We waited outside the door. I remember sitting there when the doctor came out and, with that uncomfortable mixture of fear, distance, and disappointment on his face, uttered the two words that would remain forever etched in my mind: "He's gone."

Such simple words. Such harmless, innocent words. In any other context they would have been totally benign. In my head, those two words kept dancing around. "He's gone? What do you mean he's gone? Where did he go? For a walk? For a breath of fresh air?"

And yet, with those two words an entire world came to an end.

One day I was a bubbly fifteen-year-old girl, filled with crushes on boys and hope for the future. The next day my whole life fell apart.

What died on June 23, 1978?

My father died.

I would never again feel his touch, hear his voice, or just watch him reading late at night on the couch. I would never receive his disapproving glance to set me straight whenever I misbehaved, or his guidance and support when I needed direction. I would never hear the sound of his deafening snores, which always helped me feel sheltered at night. The rhythm of his breathing was my private lullaby. I would forever miss our studying, our singing, our praying, our silences. Most of all, I would never again have my daddy, the man who always made me feel safe. I knew now that my father could not even protect himself. So who could possibly protect me?

And what *else* died on that Friday afternoon?

My mother died. The mother who had always been strong, who had always taken care of me. Overnight, she seemed weak and torn apart. People kept saying to me, "You have to be strong now for your mother, she needs you."

My family died. The man who shot my father also shot a hole straight through the center of our previously strong core. When we came to synagogue, people stared and whispered. When we had family get-togethers, the tension was overwhelming. Each of us seemed to prefer to be alone. Each of us was hurting too deeply to be able to comfort the other. We were no longer a normal family.

My faith in humanity died. I thought to myself, "How could that man shoot my father? How *could* he?" I grew suspicious of strangers. I no longer trusted anyone I didn't know.

My faith in doctors died. They operated on him, they connected him to so many machines and gadgets and tubes and wires. Why couldn't they save him?

My faith in the police died. On TV the bad guys always get caught, but the police never found the man who murdered my father. They never brought him to justice. The case has never been solved.

My belief that life was predictable and orderly died. Until that day, everything in my life had gone according to plan. Now I could no longer trust what tomorrow would bring. I started to worry about what the next tragedy might be. I never wanted to be caught off guard like that again. At fifteen I became a dire pessimist, convinced that something terrible was lurking around every bend.

All holidays died. The first Passover after my father's death, I begged my grandfather to take my father's seat at the head of the table, but he declined. "I can't sit in your father's seat," he said. "I can't take his place." So no one sat in my father's chair. It lay empty like Elijah's chair, the chair that Jews traditionally leave vacant for the Prophet Elijah's appearance at circumcisions.

Dinner conversations died. I remember the dinner table being a place of chatter and commotion when I was a small child. The mood was always festive, the food savory and plentiful. But by now my three older siblings had already moved out of the house. After my father's death, my mother would occasionally set three plates on the table and I would have to remind her to remove one. I would sit at the dinner table in silence and stare at my mother, trying to eat as quickly as possible so that I could return to my room and shut the door behind me.

The ability to walk down the street and feel safe died.

The cheerful fifteen-year-old girl I had been the day before died. How could I ever become her again?

And one more thing died in June of 1978: God died too.

The God who performs great miracles, the God who protects and defends, the God who answers our prayers. What happened to that God the night my father was standing on the street? Was God sleeping? Was God on vacation? Was my father a sinner who had to be punished? Was my father so dear to God that he had to be taken away to heaven? Was his death God's will?

There is a line in a daily Jewish prayer that reads, "Show Your mercy to the righteous and the just, O God." After my father's murder, every time I reached this prayer I would choke up, I couldn't bring myself to utter the words. They sounded like lies. My father, after all, was a righteous person. He was soft-spoken, kind, and humble. He was honest and principled and loving, a gentle soul who loved to study and to teach, who loved praying to God. But what good did all that praying do? Did God protect him when it really counted? Soon I stopped praying.

Look what one man with a gun in his hand had done. The ancient rabbinic teaching is certainly true: to destroy a single life is to destroy the world. That murderer destroyed my world.

IT HAS BEEN twenty years since my father's death, and not a day goes by when I don't think of him. I cannot make a decision without wondering how he might have advised me. Every celebration, every birth, every joy, is tinged with a bittersweet longing for his presence, his loving glance.

One strange thing about suffering is that life around you seems so completely indifferent to your condition. In the general scheme of things, my father's death was totally insignificant. Even his murder was just another statistic, just another shooting on the streets of Brooklyn. It didn't even make the evening news. And yet, his death changed me forever.

Another strange thing about suffering is that people expect you to recover, to bounce back quickly. They don't seem to see what is so obvious to you. You have not only endured a tragedy, you have lost your world.

But is this world lost *forever?* Is there no way to restore the hope, the trust, the joy, the optimism, the faith that each of us once felt? As we make our journey through this life, so many pieces of ourselves die along the way. Each one of us who has been hurt knows these losses intimately. Take a moment and think of all the things that have died: the dreams, the innocence, the relationships with friends or family members we no longer speak to, the love that is no more, the ability to be flexible and daring, the capacity to be trusting, the enthusiasm, the hope. Every one of us carries such a list. Every one of us has suffered, at some point in our lives, a hurt that has robbed us of much more than we could ever have dreamed.

"Let me not die while I am still alive," a great Hasidic rabbi once taught. What a powerful prayer. It is the prayer of all those who are in pain and who are struggling to find their way back to life. It asks God to give us the strength to resurrect the pieces of ourselves that can still be revived.

Death is a great tragedy. But to die while we are still living, that is the greatest tragedy of all.

ONE DAY HELEN, a tall thin blonde woman, came to see me in my study. She said that she was not Jewish but was married to a Jewish man and they had two children. Helen told me that when she and her husband were first married he didn't seem to have much interest in his religion. But recently he had returned to his faith with intense joy. She said that she was so deeply moved by her husband's devotion to his faith that she wanted to convert to Judaism. I told Helen that she didn't have to convert in order to appreciate her husband's faith, but she was adamant. She began taking courses, reading books, celebrating the Sabbath, and I agreed to take her on as a student. We studied together every Tuesday morning. She was the most passionate student I have ever taught. Every one of our sessions ended with her in tears. When I would ask why she was crying, she would respond, "It's all so beautiful."

At the year's end, I sat on the rabbinic tribunal as Helen embraced the Jewish faith together with her two children. Her husband sat beside her, beaming. It was Jim, the same man whose faith had been crushed by an insensitive usher so many years before.

.   .   .

WE ALL have the capacity to return to life, to recover our hope and our trust and our faith. We all have the potential to experience joy once more, to face this world with optimism and renewed strength.

But first we must face the darkness.

A PRAYER

When I am lost, help me, God, to find my way. When I am hurt, shelter me with Your loving presence. When my faith falters, show me that You are near. When I cry out against You, accept my protest, God, as a prayer, too. As a call for You to rid this world of all pain and tragedy. Until that day, give me the will to rebuild my life in spite of my suffering, to choose life even in the face of death.

Amen.

CHAPTER THREE

The Long Dark Night

THERE IS NO WAY to avoid the period of darkness that comes after we have experienced a devastating blow. It doesn't matter how strong or how successful we are, no one can take our place in suffering. Sooner or later we will find ourselves feeling alone and frightened, not knowing which way to turn. The darkness can follow a death, an illness, a broken relationship, a divorce. It can hit us after we lose a job, or when a milestone birthday arrives. For some the darkness strikes suddenly; for others it creeps up slowly.

When sorrow comes, there is an emptiness that pervades your entire being. There is a feeling of utter helplessness that comes too. And then there is the numbness of shock, the feelings of absolute unreality: *Did this really happen?* But soon the shock gives way to darkness. We are pulled down by a gravitational force so strong that every ounce of our will cannot combat its fierce power. It seems as if there is no way out. There are no exit signs, no guides, no windows, no doors, no lights. Only the thick blackness that leaves us groping, praying, for release. There are lighter days and darker days. There are brief moments of hope, but these give way to the overwhelming weight of the long dark night.

We may find ourselves feeling weary all day long. Walking up a short flight of stairs can feel like climbing a mountain. Or we may feel hyperactive, agitated, unable to concentrate or sleep through the night. At some point most people feel as if a veil has been dropped between themselves and the rest of the world. It seems as if the world is continuing on its usual path, people around us are in motion, and we are close enough to see them—but not able to be with them. Somehow we find ourselves watching alone from a distance. Friends may offer help, or a listening ear, but often they grow weary of our constant dreariness. They want to cheer us *out* of our pain—not be with us *in* our pain. Our pain threatens most people. It stirs up feelings they'd rather push away than deal with. Often, when we've first suffered a blow, friends offer assistance. However, with time—it might be a week, a month, or longer—they stop worrying about us. But it is only then that we are beginning to fathom the true depths of our pain.

WHEN MY FATHER DIED, I went into a deep freeze. I remember watching my mother, sister, and brother Danny that day. They were holding one another and crying. My Aunt Blanchie was shaking. I had never seen any of them cry before. It was strange to see them break down. I sat on a chair completely removed from their outpouring of emotion. I had no tears. Later that night, as my cheek touched the pillow, the tears came. But after that night I stopped crying. I sat stoically at the funeral and burial as if I were watching a movie about a funeral.

My Uncle Hy, my father's older brother, was the funniest man I have ever known. He even looked like Mel Brooks in his *Blazing Saddles* days. He would come to our house and within minutes we would be laughing hysterically. But as my father's casket was being lowered into the earth, Hy turned his head up to the sky and shouted to his deceased mother, "Mameleh, Mameleh, it's Yossele." In Hy's eyes, my father was a little boy being reunited with his mother in heaven. This was the first time in my life that I ever thought of my father as small and fragile. But as he was being laid to rest, I hoped that Hy was right.

During shiva, the week of mourning, hordes of people descended upon us. Some offered comfort, some offered food, some jokes and distractions. I felt their eyes on me as their heads shook silently in pity. I was determined to be strong. "I'm fine," I thought to myself. "I'm fine." And when all the relatives and friends went back to wherever they had come from, it was me and my mother alone in the home that had once been filled with children doubled up in small rooms, and with parents who constantly kissed and hugged. My mother was, understandably, devastated. I could see that she needed a shoulder to cry on, but I was determined not to be that shoulder. I was, after all, an adolescent trying to carve out my own identity and space. I resented her weakness. It made me even angrier than I already was.

My anger kept me afloat. I turned down comfort when it came my way. I didn't want pity or sad glances or hushed tones. What I wanted more than anything in the world, other than for my father to be alive, was to be treated like a normal person. Soon enough I succeeded. I seemed so normal at school and at summer camp that people just took it for granted that I was OK. All the pity and worry was focused on my mother. People would phone and ask, "How's Mom doing?" Family members would visit and whisper, "How is she?" The truth is that I was so busy running from her, I rarely took notice of the fact that she was in deep, deep pain. She missed my father so much that she couldn't even bear to part with his belongings. For over two years after his murder, my father's clothes still hung in the closet. His small black lace-up shoes lined the floor. His books lay exactly in the places he had left them. There was one book on a coffee table beside the couch with the bookmark still in place, pointing to all the pages that would remain forever unread. His Norelco TripleHeader rested quietly on top of the toilet tank. I used to love the sound of that shaver in the morning. Hearing the buzz, I would pop out of bed and perch myself on the closed toilet seat lid to watch my father shave. Then he'd click on the plastic safety cap and I'd "shave" too, feeling the vibration on my soft cheeks.

In my moments of black humor, I would think to myself, "Maybe Mom thinks he's going to make a comeback, like Elijah or Elvis. He'll walk through the door and he won't even have to buy a single new shirt."

I WAS in a deep, dark place, and I didn't even know it. I was so cut off from my emotions that I was unable to see just how much pain I was in. Over time, as the shock of my father's death wore off, an emotional paralysis set in. I was in such a rush to seem recovered that I never allowed myself the time to heal. I was so busy *pretending* to be fine that I started to believe I was. But my heart was in turmoil. And hiding from my pain only caused more pain. It isolated me from friends. It prevented me from showing my mother my hurt and receiving her comfort. My self-esteem plummeted. I put on weight.

The pain and isolation I was living with were overwhelming. All my girlfriends were busy planning their sweet-sixteens while I was falling deeper and deeper into despair. I was beginning to believe that there would never be an end to my pain.

Everybody I know who has been through tragedy has lived through that period of darkness. After her rape Michelle was certain her life was over. There were many, many days when she couldn't bring herself to set foot outside her door, or to pick up a phone and reach out for help. My mother was sure she would never again be able to experience joy. During my own period of darkness, all I saw was blackness that seemed to stretch into eternity. But I was wrong. We were all wrong. Our intense pain would pass in time. It did end. I can see that now, but I had no way of seeing it then.

PAIN DOES have an end. In time we will find ourselves standing at the other side of the abyss. And strangely enough, as we gain more distance from it, we will also come to *appreciate* the darkness and the invaluable lessons it has instilled in us.

A PRAYER

When the pain is intolerable, God, help me to bear it. When I feel lost and empty, teach me to see that I am not alone. Show me that You are with me. Help me to believe that there is a way out of this hell. If only I could see that my pain will end, then I think I could learn to live with this awful agony. Kindle within me the flame of hope, God, and I will carry on.

Amen.

CHAPTER FOUR

False Comforts

WE ALL NEED COMFORT during the painful dark night. We all need something to hold on to when we are in trouble. There's nothing wrong with that. This world that God has given us is filled with sources of real comfort. It's only wrong when we choose a *false* comfort, a false remedy, a false God.

The Children of Israel were standing at the foot of Mount Sinai. They had just heard the voice of God speaking the words of the Ten Commandments to them: "I am the Lord your God who brought you out of the land of Egypt, out of the house of bondage."

How much better does it get than that? Most of us spend our lives wondering if there is a God, hoping for even the smallest sign of communication with God. According to the Bible, these people actually *heard* the voice of God speaking to them. And this was no ordinary communication. This was a bond, a covenant, a promise of eternal connection. But just days later the people noticed that Moses was late coming down from the mountain and they panicked. They started to doubt whether Moses was ever going to return. They feared that God and Moses had abandoned them. Anxious and frightened, the people fashioned a golden calf and began worshipping it right at the foot of Mount Sinai.

When we cling to false comforts, we merely take ourselves

34

further down into darkness. The golden calf did not save the Israelites from their pain: it served only to blind them from seeing the truth. Moses was on his way down from Mount Sinai, carrying the Tablets of the Law in his hands. God had never left them, God was with them all along, but the people at the foot of the mountain worshipping the calf proved to Moses that they were not ready to receive God's law.

A false comfort is something we rely upon to deaden our pain or to solve our problems for us. We have all sought out false comforts at one time or another. And we have all descended into deeper darkness because of them.

In my congregation I listened to countless stories of people's destructive reliance upon false comforts. Each week, standing on the pulpit and looking out at the rows of people who came to pray, I would see the faces of many who had once fallen under the spell of various addictions. I counseled congregants who were addicted to drugs, alcohol, sex, shopping, food, gambling, and even work. I saw their denial, their lies, and their self-destructive actions. I watched the devastation they brought upon their loved ones. And I also witnessed their heroic journeys back to life.

MIKE'S FATHER WAS a gambler and a bookie. He bet on everything. Every day. Compulsively. He'd take Mike on a father-son outing to a baseball game and would spend the time betting with his cronies. As a result, Mike's childhood felt like a ride on a roller coaster. There were times when his family was extremely wealthy, when they were invited as guests to the most expensive hotels in Las Vegas, when Mike was spoiled with extravagant gifts. And then there were other times when his father lost everything and went bankrupt, when the mob was after him for unpaid gambling debts, when his family had to leave town at a moment's notice. Mike's mother was always tense. She never knew if she was going to be wealthy or penniless. She never knew when her husband was coming home or what kind of mood he was going to be in when he finally walked through the door. If he won, he was elated. If he lost, it was best to keep away from him.

Mike told me that he first tried to escape his feelings by overeating. He became a fat child. The next way was through money. He used money like morphine to help take away his pain. As a teenager, money was the only form of nurturance Mike received from his father. He was given lots of cash, lots of expensive gifts, and, when he was sixteen, a yellow Corvette to drive.

By the time he was eighteen, Mike, internalizing his loneliness and isolation, was being treated for ulcers and stress. In college he was unfocused, lonely, confused, and cut off from his feelings. After he was put on academic probation for getting into a fight with another student, he dropped out of school. Mike knew he was sinking deeper and deeper, but when he asked his father what he should do with his life, his father replied, "You're a normal guy with two hands and two legs. You'll figure it out."

Soon Mike started drinking. At first, it was fun. Alcohol helped him to relax and to escape his loneliness, especially at parties and on dates. Smart and personable, he landed a lucrative sales position at a large company. But his drinking quickly got out of hand. He was also taking tranquilizers to relieve stress and sleeping pills to help him get to bed. But neither the drinking nor the drugs were making him feel any better. He still felt empty and alone.

That's when the sex addiction began. He'd have sex with a different woman every night of the week. He was drinking to escape the fatigue of his work and having sex to escape his loneliness and guilt. In his mind he equated sex with love and felt that as long as he was having sex, he was loved.

To make things worse, his spending was also out of control. Even with his high salary, Mike managed to spend beyond his means. He bought expensive cars, stayed at the fanciest hotels, bought handmade Italian shirts, got manicures and massages.

Somewhere along the line, Mike started to regret that he had never finished college. He enrolled in school, but then hired someone to take all his tests for him. Soon he had a college diploma to hang on his wall, but it represented nothing. He had lots of women, lots of clothes, lots of money, but he still felt empty and alone.

As his drinking progressed, so did Mike's depression—which led him to drink even more heavily. He'd have a bottle of champagne for breakfast, drink all through the day, take tranquilizers, then come home and have a bottle of wine in the Jacuzzi, another with dinner, and a third with whichever woman he happened to have picked up that day. He was arrested for driving under the influence, but that didn't shake him up. He was out of control.

At work, he became more and more irresponsible. He'd be rude to clients on the phone. If he didn't like what they were telling him, he'd swear at them and hang up. Eventually, he was fired.

He stopped shaving, stopped taking care of himself. Now he was drunk *before* breakfast. One day he walked into a store and stole an alarm clock. He had an alarm clock at home; he took it just because he felt like it. The store's security guard caught him, the store pressed charges, and he was arrested for the second time. Mike's family found out about the shoplifting incident, but all they tried to do was to help clear him of the charges, to make the exterior blemish disappear. No one ever said to him, "Is anything wrong?" By this time the sex had stopped working too. "I didn't want to die, but I didn't know how to live either," he explained.

During a trip to Florida, Mike drank an entire bottle of

cheap bourbon and experienced his first blackout. He woke up in the presidential suite of the Fontainebleau Hotel.

When he returned to L.A., Mike got into a car accident. When the police pulled him over, he was belligerent, refused to cooperate, and was arrested for the third time. A few days later, during a date with a woman, he blacked out on the way home. For some reason Mike suspected that this woman had drugged him. Refusing to see how he could have gotten that drunk on his own, he became so enraged that he broke into her sorority house, accused her of poisoning him, and began threatening her. Once again he was arrested. This time it was for assault and battery.

Mike had no job, no money, no home, no life. He was totally lost. After having spent the night driving around aimlessly in desperation, he woke up at 6:00 a.m. in a strange motel and prayed to God for help. The next day he checked into a drug rehabilitation center. But getting his life back in order was no easy task. He was hostile and unwilling to receive treatment. Within a few days he walked out of the rehab center and went to the airport to leave town. But as he was about to board the plane, once again running away from his problems, he experienced a rare moment of truth. He realized, "If I don't stop running, I'm going to kill myself." He called the director of the rehab center from a pay phone at the airport and pleaded with her to take him back. She refused, saying that he was causing too much trouble, that the staff and the other patients were fed up with him. But then he begged, "Please let me back. I promise to do whatever you say." For the first time in Mike's life, he was willing to put himself in someone else's hands, he was prepared to listen. The director must have sensed his sincerity, because she agreed to readmit him. From that day in March 1980 until now, Mike has never taken another sip of alcohol.

Nineteen days after he became sober, Mike's father had a stroke, and a year later he died. Mike was devastated, and it took every ounce of his willpower to stay on track. He was not only struggling to remain sober, he still had some other destructive habits to break. The most prominent was his spending problem. At night he slept on a cot on skid row at the Midnight Mission, but by day he still frequented one of L.A.'s most exclusive health clubs. That's where he'd go to get showered and shaved. He owed five years in back taxes. Yet he'd still take women out to the most expensive restaurants in the city.

Gradually, Mike started changing. At Alcoholics Anonymous he found a sponsor who became the father he had always wanted, someone who loved him and wanted him to be honest with himself, to look for the deeper truth instead of living a life of lies. Mike said to me, "My family taught me that if I had money and possessions, I would be OK, but it only made me feel empty and sad." Then he added, "I thought that alcohol was the only thing that could save me, but that made me feel empty and sad also."

Addictions are false comforts. They are attractive because they do, in fact, provide temporary relief from pain. But they are the kinds of comforts that soon become ends in themselves. They don't steer us back to life, they are roadblocks on the path back to life.

KEITH IS MAGNETIC and handsome. He's in his late thirties and has curly black hair and striking brown eyes. He's the kind of person you can't help but notice in a crowd. And he's not just good-looking: he's kind, gentle, extremely loyal, and always ready to help. He's married with four kids and a big dog—which makes him all the more attractive to so many women. He volunteers his time to help the needy, and he comes to synagogue weekly for services.

Keith had always wanted to be a painter. He graduated from art school and spent some time pursuing a career in art. But it never worked out. He landed a job in computer graphics, and although he had quite an aptitude for it, it never gave him an outlet for expressing his true creativity.

One day he and his wife Randy came to see me in my study. She looked utterly devastated as she told me that she had trusted and loved Keith more than anyone in the world. When he would occasionally call and tell her he was going to be late for dinner, she never thought twice about it. But eventually his perpetual lateness started to get out of hand. He would forget to pick his children up from school, leaving them stranded for hours. He'd call and say he had a flat tire and not come home until five in the morning. He started staying out all night regularly, each time providing some plausible excuse involving the car, or a migraine headache, or some emergency at work. Randy said she knew that something was wrong, but she had faith in Keith and thought it was best to give him some time to work out whatever it was. I expected her to tell me that Keith had been having an affair.

To my surprise, Randy said that when she went to the bank to make a simple deposit, she discovered that their entire life savings were gone. When she confronted Keith, he admitted that he had gambled everything away. He had been going to casinos every night, withdrawing money from their savings behind her back, money that had taken them years to save.

Why was Keith gambling? I believe there are many reasons. He was running from himself—from a painful childhood. He was searching for excitement, for something to carry him away from his daily existence. He was hoping to get rich quick so he wouldn't have to plug away at his job. Of course, once he began losing money, his gambling got worse; he was always hoping that the next bet was going to make up for all his previous losses. But it only took him deeper into debt. And deeper into darkness.

I advised Keith to join a twelve-step program immediately. He was resistant at first. He didn't think he needed it. But when Randy blew up at him, telling him that he was going to lose his family if he didn't start getting help, Keith apologized. He realized that he had put her through absolute hell and agreed to seek assistance. Later that day he also apologized to his children for letting them down and promised to do everything in his power to earn their trust and respect once more.

A couple of days later, thinking about Keith, it suddenly occurred to me that he might benefit from taking up painting once more. I called him and asked him to meet me in my study. When he arrived, I told him that I wanted to commission a piece of sacred art. I pulled out the Book of Psalms and showed him how great authors managed to convey religious experiences in words, and how those same words have the power to create spiritual awakenings in those who read them. I told Keith that I wanted him to depict the kind of religious experience that no words could ever express. I asked him to strive as best as he could to capture a prayer on canvas. He seemed pleased and honored, although slightly puzzled by my request, and agreed to give it a try.

A few days later my phone rang at around 10:30 p.m. It was Keith, his voice bursting with excitement. He said, "Rabbi, I know it's late, but you've just got to come over here right now and see this." "Can it wait till morning?" I asked. "No!" he replied. I drove to his house and he met me on the street. Paint was splattered all over his clothes and hands. He practically pulled me into his garage.

There in front of me was a painting of people dancing. Their arms were thrust upward and their feet seemed to be in motion. It looked as if they had no choice but to dance. You could almost hear the music that was compelling them. In the foreground there was a figure of a man dancing with the others. His eyes were closed tightly, his face was wrinkled, but not with age—it was clenched and contorted from ecstasy—his expression conveyed a strange mixture of sadness and joy.

Speechless, I suddenly started to shiver. I had asked Keith to paint as a therapeutic endeavor. It never occurred to me that he might be highly talented. He had indeed painted a prayer. I hugged him and told him how breathtaking his painting was. He didn't really need to hear it, he already knew. As I left, I encouraged him to paint more prayers. He eagerly agreed.

Over the coming months Keith would call me many times at odd hours with that same excitement in his voice. I was excited, too, although I insisted that our meetings could wait until morning. His work was truly remarkable.

In the first few months of his recovery, Keith gambled on three different occasions. He confessed each instance to his family, then gathered the strength to stop completely. He hasn't gambled once in the last four years.

One day a friend of Keith's put him in touch with a woman who owns an art gallery. She came over to see Keith's work and immediately agreed to carry his paintings.

Keith hasn't quit his day job yet, but he has received much acclaim and endless satisfaction from his art. It was the true comfort his soul had been yearning for.

LIKE MIKE AND KEITH, every one of us has, at some point in our lives, sought comfort in a false god, a god who has dragged us down to depths we had never known before. Mine was a mistake made by women the world over: the wrong man.

I was nineteen, attending college, and still hadn't really come to terms with my father's death. I met a man at a social gathering who looked positively wounded and in deep emotional torment. Later that evening he revealed to me that he too was coping with a tragic death in his family. I was immediately attracted to him—his pain had its mirror image in my own wounded soul. The bond between us was formed almost instantly. We were both in so much pain that we clung to each other for comfort and salvation.

We fell in love. He graduated and got a job in another state, and we had one of those romantic and completely unreal long-distance relationships. My family and close friends were not very enthusiastic about him. I knew that. But I was so desperate for release from my pain that I tried not to notice. I had my own misgivings about our relationship. But instead of heeding them I found ways of ignoring them.

We got married. But it didn't take much time for me to see that the long-distance phone calls we had shared and the occasional weekends we had spent together had not given me an accurate picture of what our married life would be like. We were two extremely different people. We had different temperaments, tastes, backgrounds, interests, different ways of settling disagreements. The only thing we really had in common was our pain, and that wasn't a very strong basis for a healthy relationship. The covenant of marriage soon started to feel like a prison sentence to me.

Why did I remain in an unhappy marriage? After all, I was a mature, bright, responsible adult, about to become a rabbi. I could have just walked out the door. One reason I stayed was that, even though my life with him was full of sadness, I still loved this man. And he loved me. Also, I believed that divorce was shameful. I didn't want to experience that humiliation. I viewed divorce as a form of surrender, a way of copping out. I wanted to struggle to overcome our problems. But there was a deeper reason for my staying: I had already lost the most important man in my life—my father—and I wasn't emotionally prepared to lose another man whom I loved. I hadn't had the power to save my father when he was dying, but I believed that I did have the power to save my relationship with my husband.

As time passed, however, the distance between us grew ever wider. Sometimes I would lie awake at night, with him sleeping beside me in bed, and think to myself, "I can't believe this is what I have to look forward to for the rest of my life."

Then, like a swimmer lost at sea, I began to grasp for the things that could lead me safely to shore.

I started to jog every morning at six. In the beginning I had no stamina at all. But I kept at it and the running started to take on a life of its own. The beauty of nature at that hour was intoxicating. In the first few weeks, I ran with a Walkman and the beat of the music would keep me going. But over time the music came to feel like an intrusion, because I was now ready to listen to my own internal rhythm. As I ran, the rhythm of my breathing began to calm me, to lead me to realms of thought I had never experienced before. My running became a time of healing, of meditation, of prayer, of soul-searching. At the same time, it began to bolster my self-esteem. I felt alive. And in the process I lost close to thirty pounds and gained immeasurable confidence.

I was seeing a therapist at the time, but I was hiding my unhappiness with my marriage from him as well as from myself. Then, one day, I told my therapist the truth.

Revealing my true feelings about my marriage was frightening, but it was also like breaking a spell. The illusion of the happy marriage that I had been trying to hide behind suddenly vanished.

After that therapy session I was ready to stop hiding from my friends. I shared my concerns with them, as well as with two rabbis at my seminary who became pillars for me to lean on. After all the time I had spent trying to pretend that my marriage was OK, it felt so good to be able to admit that it was *not* OK, that I needed their support. They gave it unwaveringly.

Then I told my mother. At first I hesitated, not wanting to burden her with my troubles when I knew she had so many of her own. But from the moment I spoke honestly with her, I realized that I had misjudged her all along. She wasn't the weak or frail woman I had imagined. She was strong. *Strong.* She offered wisdom, support, a constant listening ear. She mothered me without smothering me. She told me over and over again that I had the strength to change my life.

Then Yom Kippur arrived. I was leading services in a small synagogue as a student rabbi. Quite nervous but also exhilarated, I was beginning to realize a dream. It was during the prayers of repentance that something remarkable happened to me. As I began to beat my breast for all my sins, I stopped for a moment and thought to myself, "I haven't done anything terrible enough to deserve this kind of punishment." It was an enormous epiphany. The voice within me spoke with such authority and clarity. I knew then, at that very instant, that my marriage was over.

The very next day I gathered up all my strength and left my husband. It was a cool, still October night in Manhattan. The city was silent. The darkness was the opposite of eerie, it made me feel swaddled in safety. I was a young woman alone in New York at night, but for the first time in a long time I didn't feel alone. I felt the full meaning of the word "free."

WE KNOW we have chosen a false comfort when, over time, we realize we are not getting better, we are actually feeling worse. The trouble with false comforts is that they cause problems that are immeasurably more destructive than whatever pain we were seeking to escape in the first place.

Leaving my husband was a huge turning point in my life. Had I remained in that marriage, I probably would have lived out my days on this earth in unhappiness and self-deception. Ending that relationship was one of the best things I have ever done—but it was also one of the most difficult. First, I had to admit to myself that there was nothing I could do to fix my marriage. Next, I had to tell the people who loved me that my marriage wasn't as perfect as I had pretended. Then, I had to come to believe—in the depths of my being—that I *deserved* better. I had to face the stigma of divorce. I had to leave a man I still loved, in spite of how destructive our relationship had been for me. I had to fight against my strong desire to shield him from pain. I had to fight against moments of weakness when I entertained thoughts of returning to him. I had to learn how to allow myself to lean on the people who could help me. I had to look in the mirror and ask myself why I had entered into that marriage. Most of all, I had to learn to be alone and to trust myself once more.

Once again I had to face the darkness. And then I had to begin to search for true comforts.

A PRAYER

Teach me, God, to have eyes to see all that is false and destructive. Help me to stay far from the forces that can lead me astray. Remind me that I have the power to shatter the false gods that lead me far away from You. The false gods that tempt me with false promises. May I learn to choose wisely, even when in pain, to choose not the path of false comfort but the road that will lead me back to You.
Amen.

PART TWO

True Comforts

There *are* real comforts. While false comforts prevent us from seeing clearly, true comforts are like night vision: they enable us to see into places that might ordinarily be too painful to look at. These comforts may not *erase* our pain, but they can certainly *ease* our pain. And they can offer us hope.

Chapter Five

Community

AN EXPERIENCE WITH loss or sadness often leaves us feeling isolated from the people who surround us. This may be the first time in our lives that we have ever experienced such deep loneliness. Suddenly we realize that our pain is so deep no one else can share it. Friends may empathize, but no one can live inside another person's wounded heart. Not even those who know us most intimately.

Sometimes when we are experiencing sorrow, our first instinct is to push people away. It seems counterintuitive to shut people out at the very time when we need them most, but we do it anyway. We turn down offers to go out with friends. We are abrupt on the telephone. We wish that the whole world would just leave us alone. We lose sight of a very important fact: there is great comfort in community.

There is a Jewish tradition that a single visit to someone's sickbed takes away one sixtieth of their illness. The ancient sages understood that just being in the presence of another human being can lift a person up. In one legend we are told that when Jacob was dying, his son Joseph came to visit him, and when Jacob heard that Joseph was coming, he was strengthened. He wasn't miraculously cured—he was dying of old age—but he was *strengthened* by the visit.

I have witnessed this with my own eyes. I have seen cancer

patients moaning in pain who became animated and exuberant at the sight of a visitor's presence.

I once had a congregant who had given up on life. He was depressed after heart surgery, hurt that no one had called or come to see him. He started losing weight and the doctors were quite concerned. I mentioned this to some of my congregants, who started to visit him. His transformation was remarkable. Suddenly he started to thrive, eating his meals and laughing again.

Sometimes, just by being there, we can actually save a life. But even when there is no hope of a cure, being there is a way to help ease someone's suffering.

There is a beautiful legend that describes God coming to visit Abraham when he is in pain after his circumcision. What is fascinating about this scene is that God goes to all the trouble of visiting Abraham but doesn't cure him. You would think that God, after all, could just repair the wound. But that is not what God does. God simply offers the healing power of comfort, of being by Abraham's side in a time of pain.

No matter what we think, no matter how it feels, we are not alone. There are people who care about us, who want to help us, and whose very presence can offer us hope. Spending time with someone, even if it's just for a quick cup of coffee, is often enough to lift our spirits. Sometimes the best thing we can do for ourselves when we are feeling depressed is to force our bodies out of bed and out the door. A change of scenery can also dramatically change our mood by breaking the monotony and altering our routine. It's not going to cure us of all pain, but it can help us to rejoin the world around us. Suddenly the world feels far less alien and forbidding.

Most people would prefer not to deal with the pain of others. That is why they may not call. But if we can muster the strength, this is the time for *us* to reach out to *them*. We must try very hard not to resent their silence. Instead, we must teach them not to be afraid of us. We must show them that they don't have to say anything profound, all they need to do is to be with us.

When we need to receive comfort, we don't have to make elaborate social plans, we don't have to fix a five-course dinner. We just have to be willing to say to someone "I need you." And then we have to let them enter our lives.

Of course, this is not as easy as it sounds. First, we have to find the energy to actually pick up the phone and reach out for help. Next, we have to be brave enough to allow people to see us in our vulnerable state. Finally, we have to face the possibility of getting hurt, of putting our trust in someone who may let us down. Is there anything so awful as being rejected when we are feeling fragile? Sometimes the cruel actions of a particular person can be so disillusioning that we become afraid to give anyone else a chance to hurt us as deeply. But we can't let one person's insensitive behavior shatter our faith in human kindness. Just as there will be people who disappoint us with their lack of caring, there will be others who surprise us with their generosity of spirit.

A Religious Community

A COMMUNITY of faith can provide more than support when we are lonely. The members of a faith community can strengthen our resolve to heal, can link their prayers to ours, and can restore us to faith. They can envelop us in caring and love.

Max Polsky is 101. He's gone blind and he's not always coherent, but his memory is as clear as pure water. He knows the entire prayer service by heart. And he's been attending services at Mishkon Tephilo with his wife Ethel for as long as anyone can remember. When I first met Max, he took me aside and asked me about tending to his funeral. Of course, I agreed. But that was nine years ago.

A couple of years ago Max stopped coming to services. His health was deteriorating, and it became increasingly difficult for Ethel to bring him. But the members of Mishkon Tephilo were not ready to write Max off. On Rosh Hashanah, after they had spent six hours praying in the hot, unair-conditioned sanctuary, a group of people walked—over a mile, in great heat—to Max's house. They placed Max and Ethel on chairs and carried them into their backyard. They encircled them and, for Max's benefit, repeated the prayer service they had just completed. They blew the shofar, the ram's horn that is traditionally sounded on Rosh Hashanah, held hands, and danced around them until darkness fell. Max knew all the words and joined in. He clapped and sang solo renditions of Yiddish folk songs, including all the verses that no one else could remember, but he couldn't see the tears streaming down the faces of those who had come to bring *him* joy. The sight of his happiness moved them more than he would ever know.

Sadly, Max passed away just prior to the publication of this book. I officiated at his funeral as I had promised him so many years before. The members of our community were present to pay their respects and to offer comfort and strength to Ethel.

Not everyone is as fortunate as Max was. Sometimes there is no one to offer us comfort. What if we have been abandoned and betrayed? What if we have alienated those who were once willing to comfort us? What do we do when we have no person to turn to?

In the Book of Isaiah, God says, "It is I, it is I, who am your comfort." I love this verse. It reminds me that God is with us even though we may *feel* abandoned and utterly alone. It reminds me that although others may not understand the darkness within us, God knows our deepest thoughts and our deepest hurts. We don't have to explain. We don't even have to say a single word. God knows our hearts, God is pained by our pain, and God's message to us is: "I am here." That alone is a comfort.

We may want to close our doors and our hearts and be alone in our pain when it comes. We may also want to turn away from a God who has not saved us from pain. But if we can, let us try to leave our hearts open even just a crack to welcome in the people and the God who are here to help us. Community is often the beginning of true comfort.

A PRAYER

When I am feeling self-pity, God, help me to see beyond myself. When I am feeling despair, restore me to hope. When I shut people out, help me to believe in the healing power of companionship. Remind me that I am not alone, that I am needed, that I am heard, and that You are with me, now and always.

Amen.

CHAPTER SIX

Facing Solitude, Facing Silence

SEEKING OUT the comfort of community can help us enormously when we are in pain, but we must also force ourselves to find moments of solitude.

We must not shut people out of our lives, but we *must* take the time to be alone. No one else can cry for us, no one else can mourn for us, no one else can feel our feelings for us. *We* have to do all of that. And there are times when we have to do it alone. Having people by our side can help to lift us out of our intense suffering, but sooner or later we must actually enter ourselves. We have to settle down inside our own skin and see what's there. It is frightening and it can certainly be depressing and painful. We may have the urge to run away from the intensity of this experience, but we must try to fight that urge. Wisdom, insight, and great peace can be gained only when we are ready to be alone.

Moments of true inspiration are rare in life, but when they do come they are most often found in solitude. The power to produce exquisite art or great writing, the ability to make new scientific discoveries or to experience God, is intimately connected with a capacity to be alone. Most great insights arrive when human beings are by themselves searching for answers to ultimate questions. It is in solitude that we can receive the answers that have the potential to change our lives.

We should never underestimate ourselves. And we must never believe that we are weak. In time we will come to see just how powerful we really are. Within us there is a strength that will surface and lead us back to life. Within us there is a soul that has the capacity to perceive the wisdom that God has embedded within our beings.

Silence Is a Sound

THERE IS a very common reason that people do not visit or call others who are in pain: they simply don't know what to say. We've all felt this way at one time or another: awkward, afraid we'll put our foot in our mouth. And so we often choose *not* to call, not to visit. Our culture doesn't know what to do with silence.

Silence frightens us. It unveils an intensity that we are not used to facing. When we are suffering, we may want to turn to a myriad of noisy distractions to cut the force of our solitude. But silence can help to heal us. It enables us to hear things we usually ignore.

I once counseled a woman who had asked me for help because she didn't know how to deal with her ailing husband. When I walked into her home, I couldn't believe my ears. She was all alone in the house but there were two televisions blasting in two different rooms, a radio blaring in the kitchen, and a stereo playing in the living room. She tried to hold a conversation with me in the midst of all this. I was dumbfounded. I asked her why she had all the equipment running at the same time. She said, "I like to listen to everything at once." She couldn't handle even a moment of silence.

I always tell my congregants that silence is a sound. It is the voice of God in this universe. When the Prophet Elijah had his encounter with God, he expected God to appear with great fanfare. But that is not where God was: ". . . And a great and strong wind rent the mountains, and broke the rocks in pieces before the Lord; but the Lord was not in the wind," the Bible says. "And after the wind an earthquake; but the Lord was not in the earthquake: and after the earthquake a fire; but the Lord was not in the fire: and after the fire a still small voice." That still small voice was God.

If we can get over our fear of silence, if we can learn to embrace it, we will soon come to see that silence is where God lives.

A PRAYER

God who speaks in silence, teach me not to fear silence. Remind me that running from pain only causes more pain, that distraction is no cure for suffering. Give me the courage to embrace the stillness, to encounter the quiet, that I might learn to hear Your holy voice.

Amen.

Alone in Nature

WE LIVE in a world that is breathtaking. But when we're in pain, it is difficult to see anything *but* that pain. Nothing tastes good, nothing looks good, nothing is interesting. It feels as if the world has come crashing down. It happens to everyone. And it *should* happen. We *should* be shaken to our core by a tragedy. But spending time in nature will help to show us that our lives can and will begin again.

There is a story I once heard about a young boy who went out to the woods day after day. His father took note of this strange habit and asked his child, "My son, why do you go out to the woods each day?" The son responded, "I go there to find God." At this the father gently reprimanded his child: "Don't you know that God is the same everywhere?" The son replied, "Yes, Father, but I am not the same everywhere."

Nature brings out different sides of us. Its rhythms are hypnotic, and they quickly permeate us. Before long we find ourselves relaxing, breathing more deeply. Taking in the sights, scents, and textures, we feel revived. Nature's majesty points us to God, reminds us that we are part of something that is eternal and infinite. When we stand before an ancient tree that has been there long before we were born, one that will remain there long after we are gone, we begin to understand that we are creatures in God's vast and holy universe of creation. Nature's grandeur cautions us not to take ourselves too seriously. It forces us to recognize our smallness and asks us to remember that change happens slowly, that splendor is a product of patience, of time. Nature's ferocity demonstrates to us that we are not in control, that there are forces in this universe far greater than we are.

A couple of years ago, after the Malibu fires in Los Angeles, the hills along that stretch of the Pacific Coast Highway looked like charred ruins. Those same hills today are teeming with new life. Nature teaches us that the world will carry on, will continue to thrive and repair itself. So too will we continue to heal and flourish in the face of whatever pain has come our way.

Rabbi Nachman of Bratslav was one of the great Hasidic masters of the late 1700s. Although history has been kind to him, during his own lifetime he was scorned by other Hasidic rabbis, and he suffered from severe bouts of depression. In order to lift himself out of the darkness that overtook his soul, Rabbi

Nachman would immerse himself in a ritual practice he called *hitbodedut*, a discipline of being alone in nature. Nature, Rabbi Nachman insisted, was the place where the soul could be revived. Out in nature, the great rabbi composed some of the most beautiful prayers to God. Here is one of the most moving:

> *Master of the Universe,*
> *grant me the ability to be alone;*
> *may it be my custom to go outdoors each day*
> *among the trees and grass, among all growing things,*
> *and there may I be alone, and enter into prayer,*
> *to talk with the One that I belong to.*
> *May I express there everything in my heart,*
> *and may all the foliage of the field,*
> *all grasses, trees, and plants,*
> *may they all awake at my coming,*
> *to send the powers of their life into the words of my prayer*
> *so that my prayer and speech are made whole*
> *through the life and spirit of all growing things,*
> *which are made as one by their transcendent Source.*
>
> *(Translated by Rabbi Shamai Kanter)*

CHAPTER SEVEN

Embracing Time

WHEN WE HAVE suffered a tragedy, people will expect us to bounce back soon, probably sooner than we are able. They *need* us to because they have trouble being with us when we are depressed. Often we expect *ourselves* to bounce back quickly; we may, in fact, demand it, but our bodies, our hearts, and our souls may insist on taking us first on a journey through darkness and rage, despair and loneliness.

Impatience doesn't make our pain any easier to bear. Just the opposite. We soon get frustrated with ourselves for not fighting off the sorrow fast enough. When it doesn't go away, we sometimes start to lose hope and to worry that this awful period will never end. People have come to me in tears and in panic because they feared that there would *never* be an end to their pain. They began to lose perspective, faith, and patience.

I remember feeling that my emotional agony would never lift. People told me that it would pass, but no one could tell me *when*. Was it going to lift tomorrow or next week or next month? I didn't know, so I had nothing to look forward to.

Healing is a long and gradual process. The Jewish rituals of mourning reflect this understanding. From the moment of a loved one's death until the funeral, we are not supposed to offer comfort to the mourners. Instead, we are supposed to give them the space and time to experience the shock and the horror of their loss. Only *after* the funeral does official mourning begin. The first thing mourners are supposed to do upon returning from the cemetery is to eat. Although they are in pain, they need to begin to return to life.

The initial week of mourning is called shiva. During that week the mourners are not supposed to work, shave, leave their homes, engage in sexual relations, or even stare at themselves in the mirror. This is no time for worrying about appearances or income. It is the designated time to receive comfort from those who are prepared to offer it. After shiva is completed, the mourners may return to their daily lives. But when someone mourns a parent, certain aspects of mourning continue for an entire year after the death. And then every subsequent year—on the anniversary of the death—a candle is lit in memory of the deceased, and the mourner's prayer, the Kaddish, is recited once more.

I think this emphasis on gradual healing should apply even when we are not mourning the loss of a life. A divorce is a form of death. It's the death of a dream, of a love, and of a life together. Losing a job is also a death, the death of our sense of security, of our income, lifestyle, status, and identity. A serious illness can be a death. It's the loss of our health, of our strength, of our confidence in our own bodies. *Every* pain takes time to heal.

We live in a culture that demands instant gratification of our needs. From McDonald's to the Concorde jet to the Home Shopping Network to the Ultra Slim-Fast diet, we want instant results. Health clubs promise us muscles in a month, plastic surgeons promise beauty overnight, television preachers promise salvation with the touch of a hand. I can promise this: we can't speed through our suffering. No psychic, no rabbi, no minister, no therapist or drug, can prevent us from experiencing sorrow in its proper time.

Judaism is a religion that is wary of quick fixes. An ancient sage, Rabbi Johanan ben Zakkai, once said that if you are plant-ing a tree and all of a sudden you hear someone cry out, "The Messiah has come, the Messiah has come," first finish planting your tree, *then* go out to greet the Messiah. We must first attend to whatever is before us, *then* worry about salvation. Every moment in the present, even a painful moment, offers an oppor-tunity for great insight.

Embracing time means we have to accept that no one, not even God, can free us from our situation. After the Exodus from Egypt, when the Children of Israel crossed the Red Sea, they thought they would soon be entering the Promised Land. But the road was long and difficult. They journeyed on foot, in the heat, through the desert for forty years. At times they lost hope and lashed out at Moses and God.

Anger is a very natural response to suffering. We are so angry, but we don't know whom to blame. Often we are cru-elest to those who are closest to us and they end up having to absorb much of our rage. We may turn on our friends for the simple reason that they are happy and not suffering the way we are suffering. When mourning a death, we may grow to resent the person who died for abandoning us. "Why did you have to go and leave me?" is a common refrain. We may also turn our anger inward against ourselves. We may begin to hate ourselves for being weak, unable to bounce back from our pain. We may find ourselves hating God for not preventing the tragedy that has befallen us, for not responding to our prayers. Just as our pain takes time to heal, so too does our anger. The more we try to suppress it, the deeper it festers inside our being.

Another common response to darkness is a desire to return to the past, even when the past was a time of torment. Anything seems better than facing the unknown road that lies before us. In the wilderness, the Children of Israel often romanticized the past; they longed to return to enslavement in Egypt. Sometimes when we feel lost, even certain torment may seem better than an uncertain future. I have seen battered wives run away from their torture-filled homes only to return to their abusive husbands because the pain of surviving on their own was too much to bear. I have seen men and women return to professions that were crushing their spirits because the alternative path seemed too long and uncertain.

But during those forty difficult years in the desert, an aimless band of freed Hebrew slaves was transformed into the Jewish people. Along that arduous journey they learned many invaluable lessons. They learned endurance, and they acquired faith. It was in the desert that they heard the voice of God at the foot of Mount Sinai. It was there that they received God's teachings and embraced God's law. Most of all, in the desert, without any place to run, the Children of Israel learned patience.

IN 1973, Frank was a man who thought he had it all: a wonderful wife whom he loved deeply, an adorable little son who brought him endless joy, and a coveted position in a bank that had taken him thirteen years of hard work to earn. Frank felt extremely blessed and never took his good fortune for granted.

One night the police came knocking at his door. They told Frank that he was under arrest and then took him away. In jail, he learned that a co-worker who had also been arrested had implicated him in an embezzlement scheme. At first, Frank was in complete shock and disbelief. But it didn't take long for the reality of the situation to sink in. He was an innocent man being held for a crime he hadn't committed. He felt like a fool, ashamed, angry, crushed. To make matters worse, his wife came to visit him in jail and announced that she no longer loved him. She admitted that she had been preparing for months to leave him and to take their son with her.

Suddenly Frank had lost everything: his wife, his son, his career, his good name, his freedom. Frank's colleagues, his dear friends just days before, now treated him like a pariah. It was as if his entire life up to that point had been an illusion. He felt utterly abandoned by God, too. He couldn't understand how God could permit such an injustice to take place. Frank continued to proclaim his innocence, but he was nevertheless convicted and sent to jail for three years.

If someone had told Frank at that moment, as he sat alone in his jail cell, that in time this nightmare would pass and that he would eventually find his way back to joy, he would have begged them to stop tormenting him with false hope.

Time was all that Frank had in jail. During the months of his incarceration, he felt totally alone. The darkness he had entered was overwhelming. He felt hollow, utterly rejected, physically and emotionally drained. He saw no way out of his predicament, and no way out of his despair. Then one day he picked up a pen and started writing in a journal. The next day he did the same. Soon he began writing stories, articles, even humor pieces. The writing began to take on a life of its own, and as a result, he began to see things he had never seen before. He discovered a strength and a fortitude he had never known he possessed. He even found the capacity to forgive his wife for abandoning him in his time of need. His solitude and confinement were overwhelming, but his writing gave him the power to journey into realms that had previously been unreachable.

When Frank's jail term was completed, he returned to society as a free man and began the long and difficult process of rebuilding his life, his confidence, his courage, and his trust. His banking career was over, he knew that, but during his days of confinement Frank had uncovered his true passion. In the twenty-three years since his dark days in prison, Frank has published ten books.

One day, after Frank was well established in his new life, he got a call from his son, who was then thirteen. To Frank's surprise, the boy asked if he could come live with him. Nothing could have made Frank happier. He and his son slowly built a relationship together, based on a newfound trust and love.

I F   W E   K E E P our eyes open long enough in the darkness, things will begin to take shape before us. We can learn things about ourselves that we never thought possible. We can uncover the wisdom and compassion which God has bestowed upon us that have been lying dormant within our souls. We can locate a source of strength within our being that is eternal and un-ending.

In time we will emerge from the dark place we are in. And we will carry with us the lessons of the darkness into each and every day of our lives.

A PRAYER

I am tired of waiting, God. I have suffered for too long and I am beginning to lose hope. I turn to You now, God, to put an end to this agony of mine. If relief is not near, give me the patience and the strength to continue to dwell in the darkness, to face this time of suffering with courage and dignity and faith.

Amen.

CHAPTER EIGHT

The Comfort of Prayer

WHEN ALL IS GOING WELL, most of us have no need for prayer. But when our lives take a drastic turn for the worse, we begin bargaining and making all sorts of vows. Is it childish to start praying only when we're in trouble? Is it selfish to expect God to remember us when we have taken God for granted for most of our lives? I don't think so. When we pour our hearts out to God at our darkest hour, I don't think God says, "Look who's come crawling back to me now." God is there to embrace us whenever we choose to turn to God.

Prayer has the power to lift our spirits, to remind us that we are not alone. That horrible day after she had been raped, Michelle would later tell me, reciting the Kol Nidre prayer was the beginning of her healing. She said it was like an awesome cleansing, releasing her from much of the guilt and shame she felt. It showed her that she was not to blame for her rape; that she did not deserve to be raped; that she hadn't brought this punishment upon herself. A simple prayer was the start of her long and painful journey back to life.

Mike insists that prayer is what keeps him sober. Every time he has an urge to drink, he prays to God and receives the strength to resist the overwhelming temptations of addiction.

Not long ago, a very ill man phoned me. It was not your normal conversation. As soon as I said "Hello?" he asked, "Rabbi Levy, tell me, does God answer our prayers?"

Does God answer our prayers? It is a fair question. After all, we are a results-oriented culture. Why should we ask if we are to receive no reply? The answer I gave the man, the best answer I know, was: "I believe that God hears. And I believe that God answers. When we pray, we connect with God's power. It may not be power enough to cure all illnesses, to eradicate cancer, to overcome hate. But it is power enough to help us *withstand* those things." God's response may not eliminate our suffering, but it can strengthen us in the midst of our suffering.

BRAD IS an entertainment executive in Hollywood. He's in his late thirties and wears an earring, and when I first met him he also had a ponytail. He had always been proud to be a Jew but was raised with almost no knowledge of Jewish religious life. Six years ago his wife Meg's father died and Brad started to accompany Meg to synagogue to recite the Mourner's Kaddish. He told me that the music of the service was his first prayer. He felt as if he was communicating with God. Not by asking anything of God but by simply feeling that he was in the presence of God.

Then something changed the way Brad prayed. He and Meg desperately wanted to have a child, but they were unable to conceive. They sought the advice of various specialists, and Meg underwent all sorts of fertility treatments. But month after month they were faced with nothing but disappointment.

It was then that Brad started to pray a different form of prayer, what he calls his "Let's Make a Deal" prayer. Brad began to bargain with God. He'd promise things if only God would give him a child. He'd say, "God, here's what I'll do if you come through for me," and then he'd promise to make a major contribution to the synagogue if Meg got pregnant. When he realized that his prayers weren't working, Brad found it more and more difficult to come to synagogue. He was mad at God. He told God, "What's the point of praying if the most important thing I ever wanted You can't deliver?"

Brad had never had a bar mitzvah. He decided that, even at his age, he wanted one, so he began studying with me. His Torah portion was the story of Joseph and his brothers, and as he began to delve into the meaning of the text, his understanding of God began to change. On the day of his bar mitzvah, Brad spoke eloquently about how God was with Joseph not only during his moments of triumph but also during his moments of pain, when he was alone in prison. Brad stopped thinking of God as a giant Monty Hall, stopped thinking of prayer as a form of bargaining. Instead, what he began to look for from God was strength and courage and hope. Suddenly God no longer seemed distant and deaf. Brad no longer felt alone: "Now it was Meg and me *and* God all trying to do the same thing." Now Brad's prayers were working. When he prayed for strength, he received strength. Enough strength to keep his hopes alive.

Meg never did get pregnant. But one day Brad woke up and knew that he was ready to adopt a child. Up to that point he had been ambivalent about adoption. He worried about the health of the birth mother, about the challenge of raising an adopted child. But that day Brad felt, in the depths of his being, that adoption was the correct choice to make. He told me that this realization felt like a gift from God. He had been praying for an answer and he got it. The answer was, "This is the right thing to do." The answer was not the conception of a child, it was the turning point of his life—a moment of pure clarity.

Brad and Meg soon learned that finding a baby was also an arduous task. They drove for miles to meet one potential birth mother who disappeared two days later. Another woman said she was interested in giving her baby up for adoption but that she needed them to wire her money immediately. Brad and Meg were so vulnerable, they were prepared to transfer the funds, but luckily, they learned that the whole exchange was a hoax. Then one day the right birth mother got in touch with them. It all went perfectly smoothly. Brad was in the delivery room during the birth. "It was unbelievable," he told me. He was standing there looking at this new baby girl as she was being washed and swaddled, and then the nurse turned to him and asked, "Would you like to carry your daughter into the nursery?"

These days Brad spends much of his time at synagogue chasing after his ever-active daughter Julia. But in his rare moments of silent devotion, Brad's prayers have come full circle. He has returned to the simple prayer he experienced the first time he ever walked into our synagogue. He pays little attention to the words of the service and just lets the music be his prayer. It is a feeling, not a request. It is a sense of being connected, of being part of something larger than himself. It is an attempt to simply be in the presence of God.

Music as Prayer

MUSIC HAS the amazing power to tame anger, to restore hope, to rekindle love, to heal, to soothe, to stir up a frenzy, to enable the soul to soar. In most religious services across the globe, the words of the prayers are set to music. The music is as varied as the human beings who create it. It may be complicated choral music, an ornate organ piece, a soloist's trained voice, a congregation joining together in communal singing, a steady chant, or a pulsing percussion beat. It may be in a somber minor key or in a spirited joyous outburst.

Throughout human history, religious experiences have been translated into song. When the Children of Israel crossed the Red Sea, they wanted to thank God for the miracle that God had wrought. They didn't build a monument, they didn't offer up a sacrifice or prostrate themselves before the Lord. They burst out in song.

Why song? Because music touches us in a place that no words can ever reach and conveys emotions that no words can ever capture. It is a bridge between cultures, between the body and the spirit, between human beings and God.

I remember watching the Johnny Carson show one night in 1988 when Orel Hershiser was the guest. The Dodgers had just won the World Series and Johnny asked Hershiser how he managed to keep his nerves steady in the dugout, knowing that the entire game rested on his pitching ability. Hershiser replied, "I sang hymns to myself." Johnny asked him to sing one. Hershiser, this famous baseball hero, opened his mouth and sang, in a thin shaky voice, the most gentle soulful prayer. As I listened, I instantly understood how that simple song had enabled him to soar above fear in the face of overwhelming pressure.

The most powerful form of prayer that I know is a traditional Hasidic musical chanting that has no words at all. It's called a niggun. A niggun is a repetitive refrain sung over and over. It can bring people to tears at one moment and to ecstasy the next.

Sam, our synagogue's sexton, told me that in his youth he'd had the privilege of hearing the great Modzhitzer Rebbe sing. The Modzhitzer, Sam said, sang like an angel, and composed holy melodies to God. When he went to one of the Modzhitzer's prayer services, he could practically feel the walls shake from the fervor in the room. Sam also recounted to me a story he had heard about how the Modzhitzer needed to undergo an appendectomy, but there was no anesthesia available. Instead, the great rabbi composed a niggun during his surgery. The melody took him to such spiritual heights that he felt no pain at all.

When I first started to lead a niggun in our prayer service, some people were a bit skeptical. I'm sure they were wondering what in the world I was doing. There I was on the pulpit leading a musical prayer—without words and without end. But then something strange started to happen. The music took over. Those who could not read Hebrew suddenly, for the first time in their lives, began to pray. Those who had been dozing in boredom started to chime in. Time stopped. The congregation felt like one single voice instead of hundreds of separate voices. And that single voice was infused with an intensity I had never before known. Together our souls started to take flight.

Our Actions Are Prayers Too

THE PRAYER of our hearts and mouths is our hope and yearning. But the prayer of our limbs—our actions—is our salvation. Dr. Abraham J. Heschel was one of the greatest theologians of this century. Not just a scholar and a writer, he was also an activist. When he marched with Dr. Martin Luther King, Jr., in Selma, Alabama, he proclaimed, "It felt as if my legs were praying." The goodness that we perform in this world is our highest prayer.

When we struggle to repair this world, to rise above our complacency and offer compassion, charity, and love, we are praying. When we fight to eradicate poverty, injustice, and war, when we take the time to perform acts of kindness, we are praying. When we gather the strength to give of ourselves to those who so desperately need our assistance instead of averting our gaze, we are praying. "I am my prayer to You, O God," the psalmist cried out. When our actions embody our truest humanity, we *become* a prayer.

Everyone Knows How to Pray

OFTEN people who are in trouble ask me to pray for them or their loved ones. They say, "Rabbi, I don't know *how* to pray." But *anyone* can pray. There are, of course, the prayers that were written long ago by our ancestors and have been codified into liturgy. But there are also the spontaneous prayers that flow from our hearts. They might not appear to be as beautifully crafted, but they are infused with an eloquence that is just as powerful—the passion of a soul crying out. A prayer does not have to be a ritualized, structured piece of writing. Anything that comes from the heart, that we communicate to God, can be a prayer.

There are petitionary prayers where we ask God to help us. There are prayers of repentance where we turn to God after having transgressed. There are prayers of protest where we cry out in anger, and there are prayers of gratitude for blessings. There are daily prayers and once-in-a-lifetime prayers, communal prayers and individual prayers. There are long, drawn-out prayers and prayers of just one word: "Help," "Thanks," "Sorry."

There are prayers with no words at all. They are the thoughts that we don't even have to utter. Hagar and her son Ishmael were lost in the desert, dying of hunger and thirst. The Bible tells us that God heard the cry of the child. Nowhere in the narrative does it say that the child cried out *to* God. So how could God hear the cry? The answer, according to one interpretation, is that there are cries that are silent and are heard by no one. But God hears even our silent cries.

Every one of us has a different prayer on our lips. Some of us cry out in bitter protest. Some whisper a secret longing. Others weep in pain. Our needs may be vastly different, but ultimately

71

all of our prayers contain the same yearning: a desire to be heard.

In our daily lives we are so often misunderstood. We carry thoughts within us that no one knows, hopes that have never been voiced, confessions that are too terrible to speak of, yearnings that are too deep to share with even those who are closest to us. And so we pray in the hope that God will listen and accept us in all our frailty, in all our need, in all our failings.

Each of us has a prayer in our hearts. A prayer of singular importance. Chances are we will only find it by opening our hearts and speaking directly to God. When the moment is right, close your eyes. Take a deep breath, and as you breathe out, relax. Without censoring or editing, look inside yourself. Look deep down inside. Find the prayer of your soul. Find it and speak it to God. Tell God your pain, your hope, your rage. Tell God your secret. Tell God what you need to say and listen for a reply.

A Prayer

God, I need to know that You are with me; that You hear my cry. I long to feel Your presence not just this day but every day. When I am weak and in pain, I need to know You are beside me. That in itself is often comfort enough. I do not pretend to know Your ways, to know why this world You have created can be so beautiful, so magnificent, and yet so harsh, so ugly, and so full of hate. The lot You have bestowed upon me is a heavy one. I am angry. I want to know why: why the innocent must suffer, why life is so full of grief. There are times when I want to have nothing to do with You. When to think of You brings nothing but confusion and ambivalence. And there are times, like this time, when I seek to return to You, when I feel the emptiness that comes when I am far from You. Watch over me and my loved ones. Forgive me for all that I have not been. Help me to appreciate all that I have, and to realize all that I have to offer. Help me to find my way back to You, so that I may never be alone.

Amen.

CHAPTER NINE

A Listening Ear

THE MOST central Jewish prayer is the Shema: "Hear, O Israel, the Lord our God, the Lord is One." These words are recited morning and night during the prayer service. They are also the last thing we say before we nod off to sleep. I pray them with my children every single night. These are also the last words we are commanded to say before we depart from this life. I have uttered them far too many times with men and women on their deathbeds. Why these words? Why is this the most crucial Jewish prayer? It asks us to listen, to look for God not with our eyes but with our ears and our hearts. In fact, it is customary for Jews to cover their eyes while reciting the first line of this prayer.

Often our eyes lead us astray. We pay attention to things that deceive us, things like beauty and wealth and skin color. Our eyes teach us to notice *distinctions* between things. When we listen, we gain a deeper sort of understanding, not just of those around us but of God, too. But in order to listen we have to be quiet, we have to shut out all distractions and learn to be receptive. Suddenly we may begin to notice not the differences between things, but the unity in all creation. We may even begin to comprehend what God's oneness really means.

There is nothing like opening our hearts up to someone who will listen. If we are lucky enough to find that someone, let the words come. It can be a family member or a friend, a clergy-person or a therapist. Sometimes it is an absolute stranger.

THE SUMMER AFTER my father died, my mother decided to take a trip to Israel; she needed to get some distance from the tragedy she was living with. A few weeks later she returned home with a suitcase full of gifts. A tablecloth for my aunt, a piece of jewelry for my cousin, a beautiful embroidered top for me. Later that evening, when we were alone, my mother took me aside. She gently picked up the shirt she had given me, held it close, and said, "Nomi, there's a story that goes along with this blouse. I want to give you the story, too." She proceeded to tell me that one day she had gone wandering alone in the Old City of Jerusalem. She was aimlessly looking in store windows, feeling lost and alone, when she stopped at a quaint store that sold hand-embroidered items. After she had been looking at the merchandise for quite a while, the owner of the shop, a plump middle-aged Hungarian woman, looked into her eyes and said in a broken mixture of English, Hebrew, and Hungarian, "I've been watching you, and I can see that you are terribly sad." Before my mother could say a word, the storekeeper pleaded with her not to leave. She offered my mother a stool to sit on, and for some inexplicable reason my mother agreed to sit there and wait until the owner was free.

When the store emptied out, the storekeeper put the "Closed" sign up in the window and locked the door. She sat beside my mother and said, "If you care to talk about it, that would be fine, and if you don't care to talk about it, that would be fine, too." The woman had a kind, round face, and the sweetness of her words matched the softness of her appearance. Even though my mother had never met this woman before, she knew that this was the right moment.

She instantly broke down, opened up, and poured out tears. She cried and cried. My mother sobbed and talked for hours to this total stranger who listened and listened and listened without any interruptions.

My mother could somehow tell that this woman had also suffered greatly in her life. Certainly, the woman could have used this opportunity to describe her own difficulties, but she never did. Not a word. She never moved from her seat, just sat there, making eye contact, sympathizing, understanding. God only knows how many customers she lost that afternoon. What was my mother to her? What made her shut down her business to listen to the anguished cries of a complete stranger? Her expertise was not in counseling but in peddling fabric. But she recognized my mother's pain, she perceived her broken heart, and she understood what my mother needed.

When my mother was through crying, the two women embraced. My mother felt uplifted, although totally spent. She thanked the storekeeper for listening, purchased the blouse that she had given to me as a present, and left the store.

After telling me that story, my mother looked at me with wet eyes and said, "I've never been so touched by such a soft soul."

The blouse my mother gave me didn't fit. But although I never wore it, I will carry the story with me forever. It was one of the most precious gifts I have ever received.

FINDING THE STRENGTH to be honest with someone requires that we take a huge risk. Unfortunately, sometimes when we do work up the courage to share our story with someone, that person lets us down.

I was in college, still trying to make sense of my father's death, when a friend suggested that I seek counseling. That's when I met Dr. Strand. I walked into his office, sat down in a chair, and waited for him to say something. Anything. But he didn't say a word. Not even "Welcome" or "What seems to be the problem?" He didn't make any eye contact with me, either. He just sat there, staring down at a yellow legal pad.

After a while I got up the nerve to speak and began pouring my heart out. He never looked up at me. Not once. All he did was feverishly write down every word that I uttered onto that legal pad. I thought to myself, "I came here to speak to a therapist, not to give dictation. For that I could have hired a stenographer." Nonetheless, week after week I spoke and Dr. Strand wrote.

One week I sat down and he glanced at his legal pad and said, "Let's see. You mentioned last time that you're having trouble figuring out how to work the washing machine." I looked at him in total puzzlement and told him, "I've got lots of problems, but laundry isn't one of them." He looked down at the pad and said, "Must have mixed you up with someone else."

I was furious. After all this time, he didn't even know who I was. Suddenly I felt as if this whole exercise had been a total waste of time. Exasperated, I confronted him and said, "You never say anything. You just sit there and take notes. Don't you ever have anything to say?" Dr. Strand put down his legal pad, looked up at me, and started talking. He talked and talked in a total monotone about things that had absolutely no relevance to my life. He went off on long tangents as my eyes glazed over. He spoke for my entire fifty minutes, and for the first time since I had been coming to see him, he ran over the allotted time. Finally, I interrupted and said, "Our time is up." I couldn't wait to get out of there. I was sorry I'd ever asked him to speak and even sorrier I'd asked him to listen.

After Dr. Strand, I became quite wary of therapists. But I fought very hard not to close myself off to all people as a result.

And my next experience in therapy changed the course of my life. It helped me to see that it was time to end my marriage.

If there is no one who is willing to listen to our anguished cry, remember that God hears our weeping even when we whisper. Even when we don't utter a sound. Even when we fake a smile and pretend that all is well, even when we choke back our tears, God is always there to listen and understand.

A Prayer

Help me, God, to listen with my entire being. When I am in pain, give me the courage to trust others enough to bare my heart to them. And when there is no one who will listen, hear me, God. Hear me and heal me.

Amen.

CHAPTER TEN

Tears

JACOB HAD TWELVE SONS and his favorite was Joseph. Naturally, Joseph's brothers were jealous of him. So jealous that they threw him in a pit and sold him into slavery in Egypt. But Joseph didn't remain a slave for long. Eventually, he became viceroy over all of Egypt. He got on with his life and he prospered. But he never forgot the cruelty that his brothers had shown him.

One day, because there was a famine in Canaan, Joseph's brothers journeyed to Egypt looking for food. They stood before Joseph, who was now a grown man and in charge of the food stores, but they didn't recognize him. He was dressed not like a Hebrew but like an Egyptian. He had taken an Egyptian name and spoke in Egyptian, using an interpreter to communicate with them.

Joseph recognized his brothers, however. All the pain of his childhood came rushing back to him, but he held it in. He chose to deceive his brothers, to pretend he was a stranger. He taunted them, then imprisoned them. He listened in on their conversations. Eventually, though, his emotions started to swell. How long could he maintain the lie? Twice he had to race out of the room because he felt tears coming on. He wept silently, washed his face, regained his composure, returned to his brothers, and continued to restrain himself.

Then one day Joseph could hold back no more. He turned to

his brothers and said, "I am your brother Joseph." He began to cry, the cry of a man who has held a lifetime of tears inside, the cry of a man who is ready to let down his guard and release his anger and his thoughts of revenge. He cried the cry of a young boy who has not seen his big brothers for so many years and the cry of a man who has grown too accustomed to wearing masks. In those tears was the pain of lost years, the sudden realization of all that had been wasted. But in those tears was also the joy of human bonding, the realization that all had not been lost; that the flame of anger had not burned away his love. Perhaps in those tears was the pain of looking into the eyes of a brother and seeing a stranger. And perhaps in those tears was also the joy of looking into the eyes of a stranger and seeing a brother. Joseph's cry was so loud, the Bible says, that it could be heard throughout all the land of Egypt. He fell upon his brothers; they wept some more and embraced and kissed.

Only when Joseph was ready to cry was he ready to be reunited with his brothers. His tears removed the callousness from his heart. They gave him the capacity to forgive, to feel, to love, to be affectionate once more.

Recently my son had a crying fit over a toy that I refused to buy him. After what seemed to be hours of screaming—in the middle of the store, no less—he finally calmed down. I took out a tissue and was about to dry his face when he stopped me and said, "No, Mommy. I want to wear my tears."

For too many of us adults, tears are a source of embarrassment. We see them as a sign of weakness or childishness. We teach our children that only babies cry. Boys are told that only sissies cry. So as we grow older, we find ways to hold back the tears, to stifle our emotions and cut ourselves off from our feelings. I always dread it when I feel tears coming on. It means that I'm going to have to give in to my hurt. It means that I'm going to have to lose control and break down. But tears help ease our suffering. They enable us to express primal emotions that we have no way of putting into words—hurt, pain, sadness, loneliness, frustration, even joy.

It is so much easier to say "I'm fine" than it is to say "I'm in deep pain." In the Book of Jeremiah the prophet says: "My soul shall weep in secret." How many of us can only weep when we're alone? Or, worse, how many of us can never weep at all? Some of us are holding back a lifetime of tears, a lifetime of hurts that remain unexpressed. Over time the hurt within us turns to anger, and the heart within us turns to stone. Tears have the power to soften our hardened hearts; they can return us to the warm and open child we once were. They have the power to tear down the wall of isolation that surrounds us when we are suffering. To cry in the presence of another is to let them into our private world of sorrow. It is an act of faith, a hope that whoever is with us will reach out and offer comfort. Crying is also an act of great courage, because we never know how other people will respond. Will they just stand there looking uncomfortable? Will they walk away? Or will they come close and encircle us in love?

In order to cry we have to be willing to experience our sadness. We have to stop running from painful thoughts and stop clamping down on ourselves when our sorrow begins to surface. We must be willing to relinquish control and unleash the pent-up whirlwind of emotion that lies within us. When we cry, our souls, our minds, our hearts, and our bodies become one: they are unified in a single outpouring of anguish. Most of the time our bodies and souls aren't synchronized. Our souls may be weeping, but our faces may be smiling. Our minds may be in one place while our bodies are in another.

Occasionally we enter a state of oneness when every single aspect of ourselves is engaged at the same moment. It's what happens when two people make love the way love is meant to be made. Their hearts, their souls, their breath, their flesh, their minds, are intertwined in a moment of holy oneness.

The same is true of tears. We can't cry if our minds are distracted or our bodies are constricted. But when the time is right, if we allow tears to come, our entire being will open up and express itself in a singular outpouring of emotion.

I have never met a person who has not felt better after crying. It's a great cleansing release. I have never met a person who has not looked more beautiful after crying. We usually think crying makes us look ugly. Your face is all blotchy, your nose is red, your makeup is smeared. But to me there is nothing more beautiful than a person's face after a cry. A sense of peace and relief settles on his or her expression. A holy calm.

We all need to learn how to wear our tears. We need to learn how to let ourselves cry and, like Joseph, to bask in the precious healing that our tears will bring.

CHAPTER ELEVEN

The Power of Touch

THERE ARE two ways to check for a fever. One is with a thermometer. The other is to rest your hand or lips against a warm forehead. Both methods are fairly accurate. But one leaves us with nothing more than a number. The other leaves us with the seeds of healing.

That touch conveys so much more than a simple temperature reading: it conveys the power of comfort, the assurance that all will be well. That loving touch, all by itself, makes us feel a little better.

In the Talmud there is a beautiful and mysterious story about a rabbi named Eleazar who was ill. When Rabbi Johanan came to visit him, he discovered his friend lying in a dark house. Rabbi Johanan rolled up his sleeve and a rare light shone forth from his bared arm, illuminating the room. Rabbi Johanan asked Rabbi Eleazar if he desired this suffering. The sick man said no. Rabbi Johanan then said, "Give me your hand." Rabbi Eleazar extended his hand, and Rabbi Johanan's touch miraculously healed him.

Light doesn't radiate from our friends' arms, but their touch does possess a holiness that can raise us up. A simple touch can lift our spirits, can bring us hope and companionship, can remind us that we are loved.

When Michelle held the Torah in her arms on that horrible

day after she had been raped, it brought her closer to God. By hugging the Torah, she was physically able to cling to God and, as a result, to find a degree of peace, despite her anger. Sometimes a simple touch can calm us and comfort us when there are no words to soothe our souls.

When we are sick, people who visit us sometimes fear touching us. A man who had AIDS once told me that he longed to be held and stroked, but that many of his friends were too frightened even to get near him. We don't have to wait passively, hoping that the people in our lives will reach out to us. Sometimes we have to ask for a hand or a hug. And that physical contact can make all the difference in the world.

I once attended the funeral of a man who had left behind a young wife with two small children. During the funeral I watched the young widow standing all alone with her two little boys. She was pale and shaking and sobbing, so weak from grief that she could barely stand. At the end of the service, I watched her as she embraced everyone who had come to pay their respects. She didn't wait to see if they would hold her. She just came up to them, embracing every single person who approached her. And with each hug she seemed to gain strength. It was as if she received a transfusion of spirit from every point of contact. By the end of the receiving line, the woman's color had returned and her shivering had stopped; she was ready to begin the long process of grieving and of bracing herself to be a comforting mother to her two fatherless sons.

As much as a touch can help us when we are suffering, we should never forget that our touch is also a source of healing to others. Once, in a university class I was teaching on spirituality, I asked my students to tell me the most powerful religious experience they'd ever had. I expected an uncomfortable silence. I thought it would take people a while to conjure up their most moving moment; I wondered if anyone would have the courage to reveal such a personal story to a class of strangers. But before

I even completed my sentence, one man in my class called out, "That's easy." He told us that his son had been born in critical condition and had immediately been placed in the neonatal intensive care unit. As he continued his story, he seemed to be looking beyond us, as if we weren't there. The student explained that he had always promised himself that if God ever gave him a child, he would bless his child every Sabbath eve. Well, it was Friday night, and my student knew what he needed to do. He walked into the neonatal ICU and stared at his tiny, vulnerable son lying before him. The doctors couldn't tell if the boy was going to live or die. The man knelt over his baby's crib, placed his big hands over his child's little head, and uttered the words of the priestly blessing: "May God bless you and watch over you. May God's countenance shine upon you and offer you grace. May God's presence be with you and grant you peace."

The student suddenly shuddered and once again seemed to be looking at all of us in the class. It was as if he were waking up from a nightmare. Then he said, "That's it. That was the most incredible religious experience I've ever had."

If you have never laid your hands in blessing upon your child or upon anyone you love, try it. You cannot imagine the love that is transferred at that moment. If you have never been blessed by someone's hands, ask someone to do it. The feeling is extraordinary. In my synagogue I instituted a tradition each Friday night. After the service we would form a large circle. Then each person placed a hand upon the person beside them and blessed them. The words of the blessing were powerful in themselves, but the physical connection between human beings was like a bridge that transferred holiness and healing from one person to another.

We can't *cure* illness with our touch, but we can bring healing and comfort and blessing. With a touch we can also mend differences, resentments, and hatred. When there are deep estrangements between friends or family members, sometimes words are of no use. We find ourselves arguing the same points over and over again. But an embrace can convey the love that lies beyond all the bickering and miscommunication.

We don't have to love our enemies in order to make peace with them, but we do have to be willing to extend a hand, a touch. On the eve of the signing of the peace agreement between Israel and the Palestinians, a reporter asked then–Prime Minister Yitzhak Rabin if he was prepared to shake the hand of Yasir Arafat at the signing ceremony. Rabin responded stoically, "If necessary, I will." The very next morning I watched in awe as two enemies whose people have spent a century killing each other reached across an abyss of fear and distrust to shake hands. As I watched this miraculous moment, I was reminded of the story in the Talmud when Rabbi Johanan reached out to Rabbi Eleazar, when a light shone forth from his arm and Eleazar was healed. When one human being stretches out a hand to another, a light *does* shine forth from it. It is a light that can illuminate the dark night and show us the path to comfort, to healing, to blessing, to love, even to peace.

A PRAYER

God, strengthen in me the desire to strive for healing. Remind me that Your holiness resides in my touch. Give me the courage to reach out across the abyss of fear and resentment and grasp the hands I need to hold. And may my touch be a source of comfort and blessing and peace.
Amen.

Chapter Twelve

Learning

When I was in nursery school, I came home one day and announced that when I grew up I wanted to be a rabbi. My parents laughed and patted me lovingly on the head the way I now do when my son tells me he'd like to be a cowboy. At the time, there were no women rabbis. My dream was not only farfetched, it was impossible. "Rabbis are men," my friend Sherrie reminded me when I shared my secret fantasy with her.

I think, deep down, that my father always wanted me to be a rabbi. I say "I think" because he never exactly said so. But every time I mentioned it, he would light up. I'm sure that a life of Jewish learning is what he secretly wished for himself.

As a young man, my father wanted to study Jewish literature. He applied and was admitted to the Hebrew University in Jerusalem. But he had a wife and a child to support, and he wasn't prepared to drag them to Israel without any guarantees of security. Instead, he opted to be practical. He took a job working in his father's clothing business, which he eventually inherited. And he derived his fulfillment from providing his children with the learning he had not been able to pursue for himself.

When I was a child, I didn't have the kind of relationship with my father that many of my friends had with theirs. Their fathers threw balls with them or took them to the park or to the movies. I can't remember my father ever doing any of those things with me. Instead, he'd take me to shul, to synagogue, and teach me a prayer or how to chant a haftorah, a reading from the Prophets. He'd come to visit me at summer camp, and instead of roaming the camp grounds, visiting arts and crafts or rowing a boat on the lake, the two of us would steal away to the library and study. One time, I was about twelve and had just returned from camp. My father sat me down on the living room couch, opened up a haftorah, and said, "Let me see how well you can sight-read this." No big deal. I took the book and started singing. When I was done, I looked up to see something I had never seen before. There were tears in my father's eyes. He stared at me and said, "Nomi, I love you."

At the time, I felt uncomfortable about the intensity of my father's emotion. After all, I was just a twelve-year-old kid who wanted to get off the couch, go outside, and play. Now, looking back on that moment, I realize how special it really was. At that moment my father saw that he had succeeded in passing down his love for Jewish learning to his child.

I soaked up everything my father had to teach me. But as I grew older, I started to feel more self-conscious about my dream of becoming a rabbi. People thought it was cute, but I was deadly serious. I felt hurt and ashamed when they would laugh at me. Over time I stopped talking about it altogether. Just the same, when it came time for me to fill out the blurb for my eighth-grade graduation book, I wrote:

Favorite sport: basketball
Hobbies: playing guitar
Ambition: rabbi

Once again my yearning drew chuckles. But not from my parents. By then they had started to root for me. My father fought with my synagogue to allow me to lead the Sabbath service at my bat mitzvah. He didn't send me to a tutor for lessons, he came home from work each night and taught me himself.

Studying with my father was an incredible experience. He showed me how to pay attention to the smallest details. How to search for hidden meaning and to trust my own instincts. How to sing from my soul. I still have the tape he made for me of the Friday night service. Every now and then I remove it from its treasured spot in my jewelry box and play it. At first I get frightened when I hear his voice calling out to me once more. But then I settle into my chair, close my eyes, and absorb his passionate prayers and his undying teachings.

In keeping with the homespun theme, my mother decided to do all the catering for my bat mitzvah celebration. She cooked and baked for weeks, then got her friends, invited guests, to serve the food at the party. My classmate Scott, who was quite wealthy and had had one of those posh bar mitzvah parties, exclaimed, "I've never seen such well-dressed help."

In the end, I *was* allowed to lead the service at my bat mitzvah—it was a historic breakthrough in my Conservative synagogue—but the rabbi refused to let me utter any of the blessings. A man had to do that. On that day, my father and I stood on the pulpit, side by side, just as we had been during all the months of my training. I chanted the service, he offered up the blessings. My father worried that his presence on the pulpit might somehow lessen my sense of accomplishment, but he could not have been more mistaken. I was proud to share the pulpit with him. And honored to have been his disciple and his child. The service we jointly led was an awesome experience of prayer, song, faith, and love. The love of God coupled with the love of a father and a daughter.

My bat mitzvah further fueled my rabbinic longings. But I soon found myself at an Orthodox high school, which would have treated my desire not as something cute but as pure blasphemy. So my secret stayed locked inside me like a hidden treasure.

But the day my father was murdered, that dream of mine died, too. I resented my religion for tempting me with lies, and I hated my God for abandoning me. The omnipotent God I had always believed in no longer seemed compatible with the tragic reality I now faced.

When I went off to college, I decided to pursue a career in medicine. But I wasn't at all interested in chemistry and the sight of blood made me nauseous. Something else was also tugging me away from that particular path. I began to realize that by resenting my faith I was cutting myself off from the precious legacy my father had left me. Religion was the arena that my father and I had shared. By withdrawing from it, I felt only further removed from him and from everything he had taught me about the beauty of our faith, about the importance of striving to change my tradition.

The following semester I enrolled in a modern Hebrew poetry class, where I studied the work of an Israeli poet named Yehuda Amichai. Without any warning, Amichai's words sneaked inside my well-defended heart. He wrote about his deceased father, his war-torn country, his extinct faith, his impotent God, and about the paradox of being a secular Jew writing poems in a holy tongue. His poetry was full of contradictions—it was cynical but innocent, biting but loving, Jewish but universal, simple but wise. And it unleashed in me a spiritual honesty I had never known before. The Judaism I had studied in religious school was all about absolutes. God was all-powerful. God's laws were to be heeded, not questioned. The Bible was to be taken as God's word and wasn't open to critical scrutiny. But I was *full* of questions. And now this poet was teaching me the beauty of uncertainty, of paradox, of protest. He was showing me that it is possible to love and hate God at once, to view God as omnipotent and impotent at once, to find the holy in profane endeavors and to find the profane in holy endeavors. The strangest paradox of all was that this utterly secular poetry had actually ignited a great spirituality in me.

I suddenly realized that it was my own concept of God that had caused me to feel so abandoned by God when my father died. I had believed in a God who intervenes in our lives to protect the innocent and punish the evil. But, of course, if I had just once picked up a newspaper on any given day of the week and read it with true compassion, I would have known that this kind of belief in God was inaccurate. Every day the headlines remind us of the innocent lives that are taken, of the children who go hungry, of the millions of anonymous suffering souls. Yet for years I retained my faith in a God who protects us because nothing had ever happened to me to disprove it. Once this world's ugliness invaded my own family, everything suddenly changed. I could no longer ignore the contradiction between my understanding of God and my father's senseless murder. It's a sad commentary about me—and about all of us who happily make our way through life without ever questioning our beliefs until reality smacks us in the face. After my father's murder I could no longer read about the horrors of this world with a dispassionate complacency. I now knew that each victim I read about in the newspaper had a name, a smile, a love, and a hope. I now had two choices. I could continue to resent God, or I could find a new way of thinking about God.

After three years analyzing Amichai's poetry, I wrote my honors thesis about the way he quotes biblical verses to undermine traditional religious assumptions about God. As I began writing, I slowly found a path toward redefining and resurrecting my own faith. I started to study the Bible in a new way, reading it not as divine dictation but as metaphor. It became a way for me to understand the most basic human instincts, a path toward deepening my connection to God and toward uniting me with my own people and history. I now saw God not as a force who could control my fate or shield me from all harm, but as a presence who has the power to subtly point me toward the holiness that resides in simple acts. Once I made that leap, I could stop hating God and start listening to God. And at last I could stop blaming God for my father's murder.

I began to believe in a God who was just as outraged as I was, just as pained, and just as helpless to protect us from all harm. The Prophet Isaiah describes God this way: "In all their affliction God was afflicted." God is not distant and unfeeling but compassionate. God suffers when we suffer. I came to believe in a God who was with Michelle in that dark trunk, who was with my father as he lay bleeding on the street. I was no longer looking to God to *prevent* ugliness, I was looking to God for the strength to carry on *in the face of* ugliness. I was looking to God to show me the way to prevent the cruelty *I* had the power to prevent. I was looking to God to show me the way to behave compassionately and honestly. Suddenly that dream, long dead inside of me, was resurrected. My years of running and resenting were over. I immersed myself in my faith and learning, but this time with new eyes.

Then something unbelievable happened. For the first time in its history, the Jewish Theological Seminary resolved to hold a vote on the issue of women's ordination. When I heard about this, I was so nervous I could barely eat or sleep. Late one night my friend Tom, an editor at the Cornell student newspaper, called to read the news to me right off the AP wire. "The Jewish Theological Seminary of America has voted to admit women into its rabbinical school." I screamed and laughed and cried.

It was 1984, and I was in that first class of women to enter the seminary, one of the very few women who had come straight out of college. Most of my female classmates had been waiting for years to enter. They had husbands, children, and careers. There was even one woman in her sixties. At the seminary I found an environment where my questions were welcomed, where debate was encouraged, where faith and protest were viewed not as incompatible but as integral to religious life. I was elated, amazed, overwhelmed. I delved into my courses with a hunger and a joy I had never known before. The fanciful dream of a four-year-old girl was at last becoming a reality.

Being a rabbi is a way for me to transmit to others the spiritual fervor that my father transmitted to me. I thank him for the passion I have for music and prayer and learning, and I thank him for nurturing my Jewish soul and my love of God. And I love him all the more each time I teach others something he taught me.

IT WASN'T PRAYER and it wasn't meditation that helped me find my faith after my father's murder. It was study. Most of us think of study as something dry or academic, but study can lead us to great spiritual insight and bring us comfort in the midst of deep suffering.

A great historian, Dr. Louis Finkelstein, once said, "When I pray, I speak to God; when I study, God speaks to me." Prayer is a way for us to reach out to God, a way to share our hopes and our hurts with a Being who will listen. But study is the way to receive God's wisdom. No doubt there is an inner wisdom that we all possess, and we do need to stop and hear what it has to say. But that alone is not enough. We should be skeptical of anyone who tells us that all the knowledge we need is already inside of us. I think that approach to healing is a form of idolatry. We are not self-contained, all-knowing gods. We don't have all the answers. No one person does. There is so much that we need to learn from those who have come before us and from those who are wiser and more learned. We should never stop searching and inquiring. We should never stop reading and listening.

We are never too old to begin to study, we are never too wise to learn something new. Read the Bible. Read the holy books of other faiths. Read history, fiction, poetry. Read the same words over and over again until their higher meaning is revealed. Read different words, by many thinkers and writers, so that the many facets of a single truth will become clear. Soon we may begin to see that our problems are not new. Our questions are as old as the centuries. Soon we may begin to hear God calling out to us from between the lines. Answers may start to surface.

I pray that our learning will lead us not only to healing and wisdom but also to action. There is a rabbinic saying that if we want to see how well a Torah scholar has learned, we don't need to test his or her knowledge, we need to watch his or her actions. If we have learned well, our learning should lead us to acts of kindness and compassion. It should point us not only in the direction of helping ourselves but also in the direction of aiding those who so desperately need our assistance.

CHAPTER THIRTEEN

Memory

MOST COMFORTS help us to ease our pain and carry on despite our suffering. But one source of comfort has the power to transport us in time *away* from that hurt: memory.

Memory can return us to the days of laughter and youth. It is the closest thing we have to whatever we've lost. Even when we are alone, without our health or possessions or our loved ones, even when we have lost our jobs, our homes, even our freedom, our memory comes to remind us of who we are and where we have come from.

Sometimes memory haunts us with painful flashbacks we wish we could forget. But memory is also a window of light in a present that is dark and stifling.

The Jewish people are a people who have survived because of their memory, their ability to take the past along with them on every journey. They survived after the Temple in Jerusalem was destroyed, after they were exiled from their land, and even though this persistent focus on memory caused them to be persecuted wherever they settled.

Once I went to hear the Dalai Lama speak in Los Angeles. He said that he wanted to find out how the Jewish people had retained their culture and faith over centuries of exile, assimilation, and persecution. He wondered if Jews possessed some special secret for keeping their religion alive. To the Dalai Lama this is not just a theoretical question. He is the exiled leader of Tibet, a nation whose shrines have been destroyed, whose people have been hounded and murdered on their own soil, and whose future is uncertain.

As he spoke, I could not help thinking how powerful memory can be. It can keep entire *nations* alive, not just individuals. No matter what we have lost, no matter what tortures we have endured, we each have the power to take all the richness of our past with us, to carry it with us always into the uncertain future.

Memory Is Our Greatest Comfort

MY PATERNAL GRANDMOTHER'S NAME was Nechama. She had heart disease and died two years before I was born. My parents named me after her—they were actually going to call me Nechama, but luckily they took pity on me. They thought that no one would be able to pronounce it, so they named me Naomi in English and Nechama in Hebrew. But the older generation of my family never called me Naomi. To them I will always be Nechumale, little Nechama.

In the basement of our house my parents kept a gigantic cardboard box that was filled with old, mostly black-and-white photographs. They weren't arranged neatly in books, there were piles and piles of them in a state of total chaos. I used to love to tiptoe down the stairs late at night, sit on the dusty floor, dig my hands into the box, and pull out stack after stack. Most of all, I loved staring at the pictures of Nechama.

My grandmother was a tiny woman. I never knew her, but I'm told she stood all of four foot nine. Everything about her was small—except for one thing. Even from the photos I could tell she had the largest breasts I had ever seen. And her ample bosom made her seem even more beautiful to me. She looked like the kind of woman you'd want to hug because you knew that in her arms you would always find softness, warmth, and tenderness. To me Nechama was the model of ideal beauty. Her perfume, I imagined, was the smell of cookies baking. She wore lovely print dresses, and in the photos she always stood beside my grandfather, who seemed so dashing and tall. But it was an illusion. My grandfather wasn't quite five feet tall. Next to Nechama, however, he seemed like a giant.

My paternal grandfather's name was Max, but we called him "Zaydie Maxy," "zaydie" being Yiddish for "grandfather." He died when I was six, but I remember him vividly. He used to swing me in his arms and sing Yiddish songs to me. We would go for walks together around the block holding hands. He was missing part of his thumb—it had gotten caught in a sewing machine at work. Zaydie Maxy made women's clothing, dresses and skirts. He had a small factory in Brooklyn. Well, not really a factory—just a few sewing machines and some racks of clothes in a two-story building behind his house. He called it "The Shop."

My father and Zaydie Maxy were in business together. Every morning my father would pack a sandwich in a brown paper bag and head off to The Shop. My father wasn't much of a businessman. He didn't like selling things. He always spoke about going back to college. Every year he'd say, "I'm going to start taking night classes at Brooklyn College." But he never did.

Zaydie Maxy had been a fervent Labor Zionist for the better part of his life, but after he lost Nechama he turned from politics and returned to the religion of his youth. He went to synagogue every morning and night. A very learned man, he was also a Yiddish poet. He occasionally published poems in the Yiddish newspaper, *Der Tog* (The Day). He wrote a poem about me when I was born. It was called, "My Nechama." When I was a child, my father would read it to me and translate. I remember asking him once, "What does the name Nechama mean?" He said, "It means comfort." But I didn't know what the word "comfort" meant, and so I asked my father to explain it. He said,

"When someone dies, the people who are left behind are very sad. If you make them feel better, that's comfort." My father told me that I was a comfort to my grandfather after my grandmother Nechama's death. I didn't really understand what he meant that day. Since then I have learned over and over again.

Zaydie Maxy lived far away from us. I remember begging him to move closer. Every other member of our extended family lived beside us when I was growing up. My other set of grandparents, my mother's parents, lived in the house next door on the second floor. I'd climb a creaky flight of stairs to get to their door, which was always unlocked. When I walked in, I'd usually find my Bubby ("grandmother" in Yiddish) cooking up something. She was either boiling chicken or making her famous apple challah cake. It was egg bread rolled up with apples, cinnamon, and raisins inside. My Zaydie Isadore was usually sitting in the living room playing chess with one of his old cronies. He would call out to me, *"Nechumale, kum aher,"* and I would come. He'd say, "Did I ever tell you that you're my favorite youngest grandchild?" Even then I knew that every one of my Zaydie's grandchildren was his favorite. I was the youngest, so I was his favorite *youngest* grandchild. My sister was the oldest, so she was his favorite *oldest* grandchild. I'd say, "Yes, Zaydie," then I'd ask, "How are you feeling today?" and no matter how sick he was, no matter how much pain he was in, he always responded, "Never better."

My grandparents' living room was covered in plastic. There were plastic slipcovers on all the couches and chairs. There was plastic on all the lampshades, even a plastic runner that led across the carpet straight through the whole apartment. When I was a child, I thought my grandparents were royalty. "Their furniture must be made of precious fabrics," I thought to myself. Whenever I walked in the door, the room glistened as the light reflected off the plastic. Sometimes I would be watching the evening news and see how they rolled out a carpet on special occasions when President Johnson returned from a trip. It always made me think of my grandparents' apartment and the shiny runway that lay before them every day of the week.

My Aunt Toby and Uncle Ruby lived with their family on the floor below my grandparents. My Aunt Leah and Uncle Nat and their children lived one floor above our family.

In our extended family, everyone barged into everyone else's home without knocking or ringing the bell. No one ever used the telephone to communicate. The mothers would simply open up the kitchen windows and scream to each other across the way. Aunt Toby would yell out her window, "Ruthie!" and my mother would come running to our kitchen window. They'd have a full conversation that way. "How are you doing?" "I couldn't sleep all night. My back was aching." "You want a heating pad?" "Sure." There was a basket on a pulley between the two houses, and my mother would put the heating pad in the basket and send it over.

Because everyone else lived so close, I wanted my Zaydie Maxy to also live nearby. One day my father came home and announced that my grandfather was moving in right across the street. We were all so excited when he moved into a tiny first-floor apartment. It was wonderful. He came over every day, ate with us, told us stories about his childhood in Poland, and put us to bed.

One day when I was in first grade, he stopped coming. He was crossing the street on his way to shul and was hit by a car. I never saw him again. Every day I'd come home from school, certain he'd be there waiting for me with his warm smile and his loving hug. But after a while I stopped looking for him.

My father was deeply sad after Zaydie Maxy died. I remember thinking to myself, "It must be lonely not to have a mother or a father." It was then that I began to understand the meaning of the word *nechama*. My father, like his own father, started at that time to go to synagogue every morning and night. Sometimes he'd take me with him. It was a small room with a bunch of old men mumbling. When the time came to say Kaddish, the mourner's prayer, they all stood. They were always very nice to me. They'd give me honey candy, and after the service there was always a kiddush, a light meal, with schnapps and pickled herring. My father always wanted me to come to shul with him. He would use all sorts of different methods to get me there. He would teach me a prayer, then he'd say, "If you come to shul today, I promise you'll get to hear everyone sing this prayer." I guess that I, like my father, didn't have a very good head for business, because I definitely should have held out for more. Who knows what I could have bargained for? But I loved the music of the prayers so much. So I went. As I joined my father at services, it never occurred to me that soon I would be standing at that same service alone, saying the Kaddish for him.

THE PROPHET ELIJAH occupies a special place in the Jewish imagination. According to Jewish tradition, he never died, but ascended to heaven in a chariot of fire while still alive. Legend has it that he now roams the earth awaiting the time when he will usher in the Messiah.

Keeping Elijah's memory alive has been a way to keep Jewish hope alive. No matter where Jews settled, no matter whether they were persecuted or exiled, no matter whether they were hated or tortured, Elijah's memory gave them the strength to carry on. The faith that he would shortly arrive and bring with him a time of messianic redemption enabled the Jewish people to withstand centuries of exile and uncertainty.

Until the Messiah comes, however, Jews believe that Elijah may pop up anywhere. At every circumcision, a chair is left empty for him. At the Passover seder, Jews leave a cup filled with wine that remains untouched for Elijah to drink. Toward the end of the seder, Jewish families all around the world open the front door to welcome Elijah into their homes, hoping he will bring with him the time of redemption. I remember so vividly the fear and excitement that would come over me when my Zaydie Isadore would open the door for Elijah. The cool spring wind of a Brooklyn night would blow through our living room, and I was sure that Elijah's spirit was with us. Just to make the experience seem that much more realistic, my grandfather would quickly drink the wine in the silver goblet set aside for Elijah, then tell us that Elijah had indeed come and had drunk his wine.

The most charming tales about Elijah are the ones about his clandestine visitations. Often in these fables a poor family takes in a pathetic-looking guest, dressed in tattered clothes, for the Sabbath. At the Sabbath's end the guest mysteriously vanishes and the family finds itself showered with abundant riches. Only then do the protagonists realize that the enigmatic guest was Elijah himself. In these tales Elijah always drops in unannounced, comes disguised as a beggar of some sort, disappears mysteriously, and leaves behind a great gift.

When my father died, there were many people in my house during the shiva, the week of mourning. They would look at us children and shake their heads in pity. Periodically, someone would come over and say, "Keep a stiff upper lip. You have to be strong for your mother." But one man stood with me right outside the kitchen. He had that thick, dumb-sounding but streetwise Brooklyn accent. Short, bald, pudgy, and wearing a striped button-down shirt, he said, "I just wanted to tell you something." I thought to myself, "Oh no, what brilliant piece of advice is this one going to have?" He leaned over, and his eyes lit up as he began to speak: "Your father and me, we were second cousins, we grew up down the block from each other. I was much poorer than he was, and he was pretty poor, and one day your father saw me looking at his roller skates. I knew how much your father loved those roller skates, but he says to me,

'Take them. I want you to have them.' That's the kind of person your father was. I'll never forget him for giving me those skates. That's all I wanted to tell you." And he walked away.

I don't know who that man was with the thick Brooklyn accent. But he cast a spell over me and, for a brief moment, let me forget my grief. Instead of reminding me of what I had just lost, he actually added to my stockpile of memories of my father. Wanting to call him to hear more stories, I asked every-one about him; I checked with every aunt and uncle, every rela-tive and family friend. But no one remembered any poor cousin who lived down the block. Perhaps he was Elijah the Prophet. Whoever he was, he offered me the comfort of memory in the middle of my sadness. He didn't try to change the subject, lec-ture me on the art of mourning, or pity me. He gave me a jewel, a memory, a small piece of my father that I did not have before. A piece of my father that always makes me smile.

I went back to Brooklyn a few years ago to celebrate my mother's seventieth birthday. It's hard to go back to the past. Nothing's ever the same. The stairs we used to play stoop ball on were all crumbling. The backyard that I used to think was as large as a football field was tiny and deserted. There was no laughter, no screaming. Even the basket and the pulley that ran between my mother's house and my aunt's house was gone. No one calls me Nechumale anymore.

I walked up the set of stairs to my grandparents' apartment and carefully unlocked the door, and as I pushed the door open I was greeted by a smell, a wonderful smell of old musty couches and plastic slipcovers, of tired wooden furniture. I was so over-whelmed by that scent that I started to laugh and cry at the same time. As I breathed it in, I was transported back to the past. I half expected my Bubby Rachel to come out with her yellow-and-orange-flowered apron on and the tissues she always crumpled up inside her dress sleeve. As I stood there tak-ing in the smells of my childhood, I realized that in the face of all our losses, in the face of the emptiness, of the gaping holes that can never be filled, our greatest *nechama,* our greatest comfort, is our memory. Our ability to reach back and remember and smile.

I left my grandparents' apartment without locking the door and went down to the basement of my mother's house. The big cardboard box was still there. I sat down on the dusty floor, reached my hand in, and pulled out a stack of photographs. At the top of the pile was a single photo of Zaydie Maxy and Nechama, holding hands and smiling. I studied the photo and realized suddenly that the photo had been taken *before.* Before he had lost his thumb. Before he had lost her. Before I had lost him.

Each one of us has suffered a loss. Each one of us has attempted to remember someone. We all long to remember what was, how it used to be before. Most of the time we expend a lot of energy trying to forget, thinking that time and distance will heal the pain of our loss. We try to distract ourselves, to keep ourselves busy. But distance and time can, in fact, be painful. They take us even further away from all that we have lost. Forgetting the past, repressing the past, denying the past, ignoring the past, is no comfort.

It's commonly said that our memory haunts us. But forgetting can haunt us more. Once I was rummaging through a drawer filled with things that had belonged to my father. I picked up a worn green booklet that had the insignia of the U.S. Army on the cover. Inside was an identification slip issued to my father when he served in World War II. The last line said, "Distinguishing Traits: Scar above the upper lip on the left side of face." I read the last line over and over again. I thought to myself: "What scar? I don't remember a scar." I started to look through photographs. But no photo had been taken close enough to catch a scar. I know it seems like a ridiculous thing. Who cares about a silly little scar? But at that moment it became a symbol to me. According to that document, that scar is what distinguished my father from other men, and I couldn't remember it.

It hurts to lose a memory of someone who is gone. Suddenly we realize that we've not only lost the person, we are beginning to forget what he or she looked like, what they sounded like, what they smelled like. We rack our brains to remember. If we're lucky, we're granted the gift of recovering what we have lost. An image returns and we sigh a deep sigh of relief and we realize: Remembering is the highest form of *nechama*, of comfort.

A PRAYER

As we make our way through our busy and often lonely days, may our thoughts lead us back to times of smiles and laughter. May our tears and pain be eased by the comfort of our memory. And may God offer us strength and comfort now and always.
Amen.

PART THREE

Fighting for Life

Comforts can only take us so far in our journey toward healing. They can lift our spirits and rekindle our hope, but they are not sufficient to restore us to life. If we are patient with ourselves, if we make use of the comforts that are available to us, we will in time begin to feel stronger—and *then* we will reach the point where we must wage the battle for life.

The Bible tells us that one night Jacob was off by himself and encountered a figure with whom he wrestled all through the night. The text is very elusive about who this being was. Was it a man or an angel? Was it a phantom? A dream? Was it Jacob fighting a battle against his own dark side? We'll never know for sure. But one thing *is* sure. Jacob needed to fight that battle in order to become the great person he was destined to be. And he needed to fight it alone. He fought bravely through the night, and at the break of day his antagonist begged Jacob to let him go. But Jacob refused until his opponent agreed to bless him. The figure acquiesced and indeed blessed Jacob by changing his name from Jacob to Israel, meaning "one who wrestles with God." Jacob emerged from his battle victorious but not unscathed. He sustained an injury that caused him to limp for the rest of his days.

Comforts can strengthen us, but they cannot fight our battles for us. Only we can do that. Only we can rebuild our lives. Only we can overcome our denial and redefine ourselves in the wake of tragedy. Only we can look inside our hearts and contend with the destructive emotions that have surfaced in response to our suffering: our envy, our guilt, our bitterness. Only we can resuscitate our relationship with God.

Healing is not something that is going to descend upon us from heaven. It is something that we are going to have to *fight* for. And the battle will change us. Like Jacob, we will emerge transformed but not unscathed. We will surely carry our scars with us for the rest of our days on this earth. But our struggle for life will lead us to a deeper understanding of ourselves and of our place in this world. It will reveal to us the strengths that we never knew we had. It will lead us toward insight, toward blessing, and toward God.

The fight begins when we can muster up the courage to start over, to pick up the pieces and rebuild that which tragedy has shattered.

CHAPTER FOURTEEN

Struggling to Build Once More

DAVID AND DOROTHY lived in their home in Los Angeles for over thirty years. Both in their seventies, David is an attorney and Dorothy a painter. Their house offered them more than mere shelter from the busy life they led. For Dorothy her home was also where she kept and displayed her life's work and passion—the paintings she had spent over fifty years creating.

Their house was a gathering place for family. At Thanksgiving, three generations came together to celebrate and reminisce. On Passover, their home was always open to those who had no family. On holidays Dorothy would leaf through the precious pages containing her mother's traditional recipes which she had painstakingly collected. She loved to use those recipes; it was a way to keep her mother's memory alive. Dorothy not only preserved her mother's cooking, she had also inherited her mother's china, with which she would proudly set her table. After she had prepared her meal and her home for a holiday, Dorothy would place a special pair of candlesticks on her festive table. These candlesticks had belonged to her grandmother, who had cherished them so much that she clung to them all through her long journey from Russia to America. After her death Dorothy's mother inherited these precious heirlooms. She in turn handed them down to Dorothy, who was honored to keep their flame of tradition and memory alive.

One day in November 1995, while David was at work and Dorothy was in town running errands, a roaring brushfire broke out near their home. Within hours David learned that it was closing in on their property. He raced back home with his son Robert, arriving just in time. The fire was rapidly making its way toward them. In a frenzy they began packing up all they could think of. The only problem was that they didn't know what was important. The house was Dorothy's domain, and only she knew where her mother's china was; where her grand-mother's candlesticks were; where her father's Bible that they had held under the canopy on their wedding day was; where the old family photographs and movies were; where all her mother's recipes were stored. David and Robert grabbed all they could until a helicopter flew overhead and announced, "Attention: Everyone must evacuate this area immediately. The fire is approaching." Quickly, they packed up the car, locked the front door behind them, and sped off. As they looked back, they could see the fire closing in, consuming everything in its path. Thick black clouds of smoke engulfed the hills behind them.

Dorothy and David checked into a hotel. They had almost nothing. No suitcases, few possessions, just the clothes on their backs. For days they waited to hear news about their home, anxiously watching the minute-by-minute reports on CNN. Then a neighbor who had managed to get back to their street called them to say, "You know how I used to be able to see your house from my window? Well, I can't see it anymore."

As the reality of their home's destruction set in, David and Dorothy were overwhelmed by two contradictory feelings. First, they were grateful that they had their lives, that no one in the family had been hurt, that all they had lost were material possessions. But at the same time, they were filled with a terrible sense of loss. The loss was more than just objects. They had lost all tangible ties to their past. Their home was gone, and so was their sense of security, of rootedness, of belonging.

After the fires had been extinguished and it was safe to return, David and Dorothy and their children set out on a drive they had made every single day of their lives. But now their neighborhood lay in ruins. The green hillside was blackened and charred, smoke rose from the stumps of tree trunks, the stench of acrid smoke filled the air. It felt as if they were driving through the end of the world.

When they approached their property, they passed the gnarled trunks of trees that had once offered shade and peace. Then they looked to where their home had stood. Nothing was left. A firefighter told them that in the midst of the raging fire the house had exploded. It had been consumed in twenty seconds. Flames had shot up 150 feet in the air, reaching a temperature of 2,000 degrees.

They began to sift through the ashes hoping to recover heirlooms and other treasured belongings, hoping that *something* might have survived intact. Different objects could be discerned by the color of the ashes they left behind. The dark hard charcoals were Dorothy's gold jewelry. Where the tall bookcases holding a lifetime of treasured books had stood, there was a pile of fine white ash. A few pages were left on the ground, but the minute anyone touched them they would disintegrate. It was a cruel treasure hunt. The candlesticks that had been kindled each Friday night for three generations had melted. Fifty years of Dorothy's paintings had been reduced to dust. Nothing remained except for the ashes that covered their clothes and choked their lungs. Then their son Robert picked something up out of the ashes and cupped it in his palm. He turned to Dorothy and said, "Mom, look what I've found." As he unclenched his palm, Dorothy gasped, then burst out crying. It was the mezuzah—the small encased scroll that Jews hang on their doorposts. Like the bush that showed Moses the way back to God, the mezuzah had burned but had not been consumed. The entire family stood frozen in shock. And then

Dorothy said, "This is it. This is where we start over. Our search has ended."

The miracle of the mezuzah that didn't burn showed Dorothy that although her home was physically lost, spiritually it was still standing. No one could take away the memories. No fire could consume her faith or her history. And because of that knowledge, Dorothy realized that she could start over again. This mezuzah had survived to remind her that she would build again.

No matter what we have lost in our lives, there is always something that survives to start over with. There is always some shard, some shred of hope, some way to begin again. Life is fragile and unpredictable, it does not always go the way we'd like it to go. We only have to look as far as our own lives to know that this is true. All that we own can be taken away in an instant. But we all have the power to start over, to trust again, and to rebuild, to carry our faith in our hearts wherever our journey takes us.

In time, after we have confronted the darkness and gained strength from comforts, we must begin the process of rebuilding our lives. It is never easy, it can certainly feel overwhelming. When the task seems *too* overwhelming, people often feel as if there is no place to start from. And that is exactly the first question we must ask ourselves—"Where do I begin?"—if we are to learn to start over.

The Prophet Jeremiah was the spiritual leader of Israel during one of its most tragic times. The people were sent into exile, their land was overrun by the Babylonians, and their holy Temple was left in ruins. What was Jeremiah supposed to say to them? How was he to offer hope and solace to a people sitting in mourning over its homeland?

It was in the midst of this time of devastation, as the Jews sat paralyzed and in shock, focusing only on the memory of their beloved holy city, that Jeremiah delivered the following message: "Build houses and live in them, plant gardens and eat their fruit. Take wives and beget sons and daughters; and take wives for your sons, and give your daughters to husbands, that they may bear sons and daughters." Jeremiah commanded the people to start living again. He insisted that, even in the midst of mourning, they must cling to life. Although their inclination was to give up, Jeremiah instructed them to build.

Why was Jeremiah so opposed to despair? Why was it so wrong for people to sit in mourning over their homeland? What if they preferred to spend the rest of their days in mourning? Who's to say it's a crime? Life is too precious a gift to waste, Jeremiah insisted. His life was dedicated to teaching people that we have no right to squander this precious gift, even when it feels like an unwanted gift, even if at times we prefer death to life. We must *treasure* life and embrace it. We must *choose* life— even when it presents us with pain. Even in exile we must find the strength to build a new home, remake our lives, and hope for better. We must start the process of renewal ourselves.

Jeremiah's message is that we can start over even if we have lost everything that was once dear to us. All of us will, at some point, suffer a tragedy. But we must all face the same question: When will life begin again?

Since the fire, David and Dorothy have built their new home on the very site where their first home once stood. People often ask them why they've chosen to move back to the same spot. Aren't they afraid of future fires? But David and Dorothy always respond that to walk away from their property would be an admission of defeat. And they are *not* defeated. They are scared, there's no denying that. Every time they smell smoke, even if it's just the smoke from a fireplace, it sends shivers down their spines. But they have rebuilt their lives in the face of their fears. And they have hung their miraculous mezuzah on their front doorpost to remind them of the fire that destroyed their home and of the faith that gave them the strength to rebuild it.

A PRAYER

Please, God, help me to recognize my frailty. May I always remember that no matter how far I have fallen, no matter how bleak my life may seem, no matter how lost I may feel, I can always begin again.

Amen.

CHAPTER FIFTEEN

Learning to Face
the Truth

WE CANNOT rebuild our lives until we are ready to acknowledge that something is broken.

Some people respond to misfortune by refusing to accept it. There are certainly times when determination leads us to overcome great adversity. But there are other times when believing that we have the power to change our fate actually *contributes* to our suffering. Sometimes the only way to heal ourselves is to accept the very truth we have been attempting to deny.

Unfortunately, there are difficult problems in life that we will never be able to solve or circumvent, no matter how much effort we invest. There are situations that will refuse to bend to our desires. What are we to do when there is no way to have dominion over our affliction?

I WAS TWENTY-THREE and in my third year of rabbinical school. I had chosen an internship in pastoral counseling and was sitting in a room alone waiting for my first client to appear. I had never counseled anyone before. Nervous, I felt young and inexperienced—because, basically, I was. I wondered what I would be asked. And how I would respond. I had replaced my well-worn jeans with a skirt and jacket to make me look the part. But it was difficult to *feel* the part, to even imagine myself as a rabbi. Even in my own mind, the title "rabbi" conjured up an image of an old man with a long beard, and here I was a young woman.

The door opened and a woman in her late twenties walked in. She had greasy black hair and thick eyeglasses—which she wore upside down. Behind the glasses, her eyes were distant and unfocused. She shuffled her feet as she walked, her arms hung limply at her sides, and there were headphones over her ears. As she got closer, I could see that the headphones weren't plugged into any radio.

I had been expecting someone to come through the door with some sort of spiritual or philosophical problem. I hadn't been expecting to encounter someone quite so disturbed. She sat down, and I took a deep breath and said, "Welcome, Sarah. How can I help you?" She said, rather sullenly, "I don't know." "Then why are you here?" I asked. Her answer was, "Because my parents are making me come." Over the next half hour Sarah explained that her parents constantly accused her of being lazy and rebellious and also harangued her to get a job and to get married. I did very little talking. At the end of our session we agreed to meet again the following week. As she left, Sarah turned to me and said, "Don't touch that dial. We'll be right back after these messages."

It was quite obvious that Sarah had a serious mental illness. I didn't know the exact diagnosis, but I was sure of one thing: This was no simple spiritual crisis. When I reported back to my supervisor, she said, "You're right. Sarah is a paranoid schizophrenic." "And how am I supposed to help her?" I wanted to know. She replied, "I'm not sure yet. Just report to me after every session. Maybe it's her parents that need your help."

The next week Sarah came in with an extra set of headphones. "These are for you," she said, and handed them to me. I thanked her for the gift and then asked why she wore them. She said, "Because it's so noisy in this city. I need to shut out the noise." I asked her, "Why do you think it is that most people in New York don't wear headphones all day?" She said, "I don't know. I think they're all crazy. Look at all those people riding on the subways. It's so loud you can't even hear yourself think." I said, "Maybe you're just more sensitive to noise than other people are." She said, "Yeah, I hear lots of strange things." Then she proceeded to tell me about the voices she heard. She told me that her father spoke to her in her head. They would be sitting in the same room and she would hear her father say something, even though his lips hadn't moved. When she'd ask her father about what he had just said, her father would reply that he hadn't spoken. When our time was up, Sarah turned to me and said, once again, "Don't touch that dial. We'll be right back after these messages."

As the weeks passed, I found myself becoming more and more interested in Sarah's strange world. When I asked her why she wore her glasses upside down, she explained that when she wore them right side up, everything around her seemed upside down. When she wore them upside down, the world around her returned to "normal."

One day I said to Sarah, "I know you feel the need to wear your headphones outside because it's too noisy for you. But is it too noisy for you here in this room where we're sitting?" She thought a moment, said "No," then reached up and removed them. I felt as if we had made a huge breakthrough. She seemed willing to listen and to trust me. I asked her the question I had asked on the first day we had met: "How can I help you?" This time Sarah responded, "Talk to my parents. Tell them I'm not lazy." I agreed to meet with them.

The very next week an elderly couple entered the room. The wife spoke up first and said, "Our Sarah has been coming here for weeks now. How come she's not better?"

I asked what they had expected to happen, and all the mother did was plead with me to try to persuade Sarah to be less stubborn. When I tried to explain to her that Sarah was not a bad girl, that she was in fact a sick woman, she wouldn't hear of it. "She's just lazy and stubborn," she insisted. Her husband chimed in and said, "She's rebellious, that's all. She just wants to give us heartache."

I told them that I did not believe Sarah's problem was a matter of will at all, that I believed she was quite ill. The father became visibly angry and the mother began to cry. She said, "You know, Rabbi, we started off penniless and then we struggled to build a business, and we did it. If you try hard enough, you can do anything. So don't tell me that she can't get better. If she wants to get better, she *will* get better." I gently said to her, "Sometimes in life there are situations that are out of our hands. I wish your daughter was just misbehaving, but she isn't. If you want to help her, you have to stop blaming her and start seeing that she needs psychiatric attention." But the parents could not accept the horrible truth: This situation was not only out of their control, it was out of Sarah's control, too. In this case, their denial, which they saw as strength, didn't help Sarah: it hurt her. It prevented her from receiving the psychiatric care she so desperately needed.

OFTEN WE PLACE far too much emphasis on the power of the will. The assumption that we have ultimate power to determine our fate seems almost like a form of idolatry. There are books that tell us we can cure our cancer if we only adopt the right mind-set. I am all for empowering people to fight for life. But what are the implications of that message for people on their deathbeds? That they *failed*? That if only they had tried harder they would have beaten the cancer cells into submission?

Likewise, there are forms of depression that no force of will can cure. In such cases our greatest act of will is to realize that our healing is not completely in our power, that we must seek out medical treatment.

Nathan came to see me one day to tell me that he was in love with one of the women in my congregation. I told him that I was happy for him, but I noticed that for a man who said he was in love he didn't seem very happy. He proceeded to explain why. Nathan had dated this woman a few times, but she soon rejected him. I knew her, and I knew she was dating someone else in my synagogue. But Nathan had become obsessed. He kept calling and sending flowers and cards. He was sure that the two of them were meant for each other. But there was nothing in the woman's actions that would lead a person to believe such things. She didn't return his phone calls, she was dating other men, she didn't love him. And when she gave him even the slightest hint of attention, he took it to mean that there was hope for a reconciliation. He was certain that deep down she loved him just as much as he loved her. That's why Nathan had come to see me, he explained. He wanted to know if I could talk to her and persuade her to date him again. I told Nathan that I didn't consider it my place to tell people whom to date.

There was no hope for him, and I knew it. All I could do was to tell him that sometimes we can want something with all our hearts, we can expend all our energy trying to achieve it, and still things won't go our way. Eventually, he took my advice. He took a year and traveled through Europe, and when he returned he was ready to move on with his life.

Julie was a regular visitor to my study. She kept coming because she wanted to know how to win her father's love. He had always been cold, critical, and uncaring, and she was determined to break through his defenses. For once she wanted to know what it was like to feel a father's love. But every time Julie confronted him, she walked away frustrated and hurt. Every phone call, every visit, left her feeling more lonely than before. I spent months counseling Julie, telling her that it is admirable to want to repair a relationship, but that sometimes we have to let go. We can't force another person to change or to love. All we can do is to accept what is before us and to try to make the best of a bad situation. Over time Julie learned to stop searching for a transformation in her father. And this new approach brought her great relief. She was able to stop searching for something she would never find, and to start looking for comforts where they could be found—in other family members, in friends, in community, in her very self.

There are things at play in this universe that are simply beyond our control. There are tragedies that will come our way in life that no amount of effort or preparation can circumvent. There are illnesses and handicaps and forces of nature that we will never be able to conquer. This is not to say we should just give in to life without a struggle. Not at all. But we do have to learn when to fight to change our situation and when to accept our lot, even if it is unfair or even cruel.

Denying reality does not really shield us from pain. It merely prevents us from moving forward; it prolongs self-defeating behaviors. Only when I began to admit to myself that I had no power to save my awful marriage was I ready to move on with my life. Only when we are prepared to accept things as they are can we begin to see ways to improve our lives.

There are times when we have to learn to relinquish control. There are even times when we have to welcome death.

The Talmud tells a powerful story about the death of one of the greatest rabbis. When Rabbi Judah the Prince was dying, all his disciples gathered around him and prayed for their master to live. They refused to accept the fact that their teacher would be taken from them. At the very same time, the angels in heaven prayed that the great rabbi would at last be released from his earthly existence to dwell among them. Rabbi Judah's house servant, hoping that the rabbi would not die, climbed up to the roof and prayed: "May the prayers of the mortals overwhelm the prayers of the angels." However, when she returned to the rabbi's sickbed and saw his torment, she changed her prayer to: "May the prayers of the angels overwhelm the prayers of the mortals." But the rabbi would not die as long as his disciples kept praying. So the maid took a pitcher and smashed it on the ground. Stunned by the sudden crash, the disciples stopped praying for an instant. At that moment Rabbi Judah's soul was at last freed from his tortured body.

It's easy to understand why Rabbi Judah's disciples prayed for him to live on. His passing would devastate them. But ultimately, it was the prayer of a simple maid that prevailed, the prayer of a maid who was prepared to face her pain and allow Rabbi Judah's suffering to come to an end.

There are times when we must search for the courage to embrace death instead of fighting it. Giving up that struggle can lead to enormous relief—both for the dying person and for those who are closest to him or her. Only then can they begin the process of closure, of saying their goodbyes and expressing gratitude for all the wonderful moments they shared together.

Embracing Chaos

THE BIBLE TELLS US that the universe grew out of chaos. It was out of chaos that God brought forth every living thing. And this world that God created is not a world of perfect order. Quite the opposite. It is a world filled with unpredictables, with upheavals in nature, with the fickleness of the human spirit. There was one occasion, the Bible tells us, when God attempted to impose order upon creation. God looked at all that had been created and saw that nothing had turned out as planned. Disgusted with humanity, God decided to destroy the world and start over again with perfect order, with Noah and the ark and every animal two by two. Ultimately, the message of the Flood story is that perfect order *can't* be found in the world of living things. Perfect order can only be found in death. Once life enters the picture, so does chaos.

I have a friend named Alan Garfinkel who is a professor of medicine at UCLA. His area of research is chaos theory. Alan once showed me pictures of two different brain waves. One was so pretty. It displayed a very symmetrical pattern of a wave followed by a point; a wave, then a point. The other was an absolute mess—ugly lines running all over the place. He asked me, "Naomi, which brain wave would you rather have?" I said, "The orderly one, of course." He said, "Not a good idea. A regular, orderly brain wave is always a sign of pathology. It's a sign of a sick brain." In fact the smooth, steady brain wave he had shown me, the one I had chosen, was a picture of an epileptic seizure. The random chaotic wave was a picture of normal, healthy brain activity. Life is a mess.

Whenever I lead services in a synagogue, there are sure to be children running up and down the aisles. It often gets pretty rowdy in the sanctuary; occasionally people complain. They can't stand the noise and the commotion. The sanctuary is no place for kids, they say. But from my perspective, a house of God that rings out with the cries of children is like that messy brain wave. As chaotic as it is, it's a sign that all is well. It's a sign of life.

Every woman who has been pregnant knows what it means to have no control. For nine months your body is hijacked by a strange being who kicks, squirms, grows, and sucks all the energy right out of you. When I was pregnant, I was plagued with terrible morning sickness. I quickly learned that morning sickness is a misnomer—it actually lasts all day—and that trying to control it is next to impossible. I tried just about everything. At first I tried to assert the power of the mind over the power of the stomach. You can imagine who won that battle. Then I enlisted the advice of just about every member of my congregation. Each day, as I came to work, there was another remedy waiting for me on my desk. I tried Tums, papaya extract, crackers, herbal teas, Chinese herbs, acupressure, two different types of acupuncture. I tried wearing bands around my wrists. I tried eating small meals, then large meals. Then the pieces of advice started to conflict with one another. One person would say, "Whatever you do, don't eat dairy products." Another would say, "Trust me, eat only cheese." I spent five months experimenting with remedies and then promptly bringing them up. Until one day I realized that the remedies were wearing me out. As each one failed to produce the desired result, I began to despair. More important, my fixation with trying to cure my nausea was robbing me of the joy of my pregnancy. When I stopped trying to cure myself, I suddenly felt an enormous sense of relief. The relief I felt wasn't a cure for nausea, it was an acknowledgment of the mysterious and awesome miracle taking place within me.

To live in this world is to embrace life in all its disarray. We must learn to accept situations that don't go according to our wishes. We also have to learn to accept the chaos that people add to our lives. Being in a relationship with any human being forces us to realize that people rarely act the way we'd like them to.

When all we can think about is how we'd like to change things, we lose our ability to appreciate things as they really are. We have to learn to accept people completely, with all their physical imperfections, their tics and strange habits, with all the marvelous quirks that make us who we are.

And isn't this true of our relationship with God? We pray to God as if we had the power to *control* God. We get angry or disillusioned because God doesn't do what we expect God to do, because God doesn't obey us or heed our requests. But what if God is not just a genie? What if our every wish is not God's command? A relationship with God means being able to accept

God in all of God's mystery. We constantly hope that God will accept *us* in all our frailty, in all our contradictions, in all our idiosyncrasies. Can we not learn to see that God *too* is filled with contradictions and paradoxes and mysteries?

The things that are beyond our control are often painful and tragic. But there is another side to chaos. We live in a world as vast and changeable as the human beings who inhabit it. As frustrating as that can be, it can also be a source of great comfort, even of great inspiration. Because a world where *anything* can happen is also a world where *great* things can happen. A world where love can surprise us when we weren't even looking for it, where kindness can come from the least likely places, where great and unexpected discoveries can be made that can cure illnesses and preserve life, where war can give way to the possibility of peace. We live in a world where miracles can happen. Where our hurts can be healed, our labors can bear fruit, where our dreams of a better world can sometimes come true.

A PRAYER

God, I have been running and hiding and I am weary. Help me to face the awful truth that I can no longer deny. Remind me that ignoring my pain will never make it disappear. Give me the courage to confront what I have so feared, the strength to endure what I cannot escape. Be with me. Guide me. Never forsake me.

Amen.

CHAPTER SIXTEEN

Redefining Ourselves

I HAVE ALWAYS regarded Shari as the epitome of the nineties woman. Successful, outgoing, and ambitious, she's a loving wife and devoted mother as well as an activist and a lobbyist for children's causes. She's a marathon runner, mountain biker, and gymnast, with an athlete's physique and a soft, pretty face.

I had seen Shari just before I went on maternity leave. She was pregnant, too, and seemed to be having a wonderful pregnancy. She was as fit as ever, and all smiles.

In mid-November Shari was in her ninth month of pregnancy. Knowing that she was carrying a baby boy, she and her husband Michael had already decided that his name would be Daniel. Their first son, Noah, was so excited about having a kid brother to play with that he began having long conversations with Daniel through Shari's tummy.

Shari went to see her obstetrician five days before her due date for her final exam. The doctor told her the baby was looking great, then asked her if she wanted to induce labor for the sake of convenience. Michael thought this was a terrific idea because he could time the circumcision to coincide with the Thanksgiving holiday. Shari was completely against it. "Let's let nature take its course," she insisted.

Shari felt wonderful and looked positively radiant. Even at this late stage of her pregnancy, she was still full of energy, and still taking a prenatal exercise class. She was so proud of her round belly that drew good wishes from everyone she met.

On Saturday, her due date, Shari went into labor. She had been through this routine when Noah was born, so she wasn't frightened. At one or two in the morning she started to have strong contractions that began coming on faster and faster. She and Michael raced to the emergency room. Shari was filled with a mixture of intense pain and excitement. A nurse hooked up the fetal monitor around her belly, then moved it from one place to another. But she couldn't seem to find the baby's heartbeat. "Don't worry," the nurse explained. "Sometimes it's just hard to find." A resident saw that the nurse needed some help and turned on an ultrasound machine. She squeezed the gel on Shari's belly, guided the ultrasound probe about, and stared at the screen. Shari was watching, too. She remembered her previous ultrasound when her doctor had struggled to capture a steady image of her son because he was constantly in motion. The baby on the screen was perfectly still. Now there was a crowd of people standing around her and Shari had a terrible gut feeling, the kind you have when you know something is going horribly wrong. But no one would say anything to her. Finally, she looked up at the doctor and said, "Is my baby dead?" The doctor replied, "Yes." And then all the people around her dispersed.

"This can't be happening," Shari kept saying over and over. She felt as though she was caught in a nightmare and all she needed to do was wake up, but the cold reality was right before her. And the intense agony of labor was getting ever worse. A nurse took her to a labor-and-delivery room. Soon her obstetrician arrived and expressed extraordinary concern, both medical and emotional. Then she checked Shari and told her that she was fully dilated and that the baby was on its way. The nurse was so shaken that she couldn't find anything the doctor asked for. Not even a simple anesthetic.

Shari was expecting her baby to be deformed. She couldn't imagine that a perfectly formed baby could be born dead. Then one final push and she saw him. "He looks perfect," was all she said when he came forth from her.

Daniel was born into silence. There were no cheers of joy from the onlookers. Not a cry, not a whimper escaped Daniel's tiny red lips.

Shari's obstetrician explained to her that the umbilical cord had compressed around Daniel's neck and that was the likely cause of death.

A nurse swaddled him in a blanket, covered his head with a tiny pink and blue hat, and handed him to his parents. Michael and Shari held him for a long while, then they handed him back to the nurse, who took him away, but not to the hospital's nursery.

Then the nurse returned and presented them with Daniel's birth record. It had his tiny footprints on it, along with his height and weight. The time of his birth and the time of his death were listed as the same.

NEXT CAME the requisite phone calls to family members and dear friends who were waiting anxiously for the news. Shari spoke to her mother and cried, "The baby's dead."

In the morning a counselor from the hospital's bereavement team came to the hospital room. She held Shari tightly and said, "Go ahead and cry," which is exactly what Shari did. The woman said that she knew a little bit of what Shari was going through, she had lost a baby too. The first question Shari asked the counselor was: "When can I get pregnant again?" The woman looked at her and said, "I know what you're trying to do. You're trying to get it right." And then she explained to Shari that she had to give herself time to heal, both physically and emotionally—at least six months to a year.

Shari was caught in a whirlwind of emotions. She felt deeply sad, helpless, guilty, powerless, and angry. She didn't know how she had fallen into this vortex or, worse, how she would ever get out.

When she was discharged from the hospital, Michael drove up in their car. As Shari got in, she saw the infant car seat propped up in the back, empty and silent.

The day after she gave birth, a time when most mothers find themselves surrounded by flowers and gifts, Shari found herself at the cemetery trying to decide what casket to use and where they wanted to have their baby buried.

Unfortunately, I was on maternity leave and out of town at the time of Shari's tragedy. She called Rabbi Neal Weinberg, who had presided over her conversion to Judaism, and asked him to perform the funeral. Rabbi Weinberg gently told Shari that traditionally the Jewish laws of mourning don't apply to a baby who dies before it reaches thirty days. Shari was indignant. She said, "I want to treat my baby like a real person." Rabbi Weinberg was extremely sensitive to her needs and performed a service that was both moving and comforting.

On the day of the funeral Shari said that Daniel looked like a baby sleeping peacefully in his cradle, not his casket. But when she touched him, his skin was so cold that she recoiled in shock. Shari didn't want her last encounter with Daniel to be one where she withdrew from him in fear, so after the service she demanded to have the casket opened once more, then she leaned over his forehead and tenderly kissed Daniel farewell.

When Shari and Michael returned home after the funeral, they felt sheltered by the love of family and friends who surrounded them. One close friend of Shari's was in her ninth month of pregnancy at the time. She came up to Shari and gave her a long loving hug. Shari could feel her friend's large belly press against her own empty belly, and she was grateful to her friend for not staying away, for not being afraid to come close to her.

The words Shari had spoken at her last visit to her obstetrician came back now to haunt her. "Let's let nature take its course," she had said. Nature *had* taken its course. Most of the time we think the word "nature" implies something healthy, positive, and life-giving. But death is also part of nature's awesome cycle. Death is the prognosis for every single living thing.

The day after the funeral, nature continued on its course. Shari's milk started to come in and there was nothing she could do to stop it. Her body was prepared to nourish a child but there was no child to suckle. There she was, lying in the bathtub with milk flowing freely from her breasts into the warm bathwater.

That night Shari walked into Daniel's room, looked at his empty crib adorned with bedding, and flew into a rage. It was three in the morning, but she ran, got a screwdriver, took the crib apart, then dragged it piece by piece into the garage. The sheer physical exertion helped her to release her anger.

Wherever she went, Shari now found herself having to explain what had happened. Whenever she told anyone about Daniel's death, people would get so upset that Shari inevitably found herself comforting them. "It's all right, we'll be OK," she would say. And then there were the insensitive pieces of advice that she was offered, such as "Just get over it, you can have more kids."

Shari was filled with anger but had no one to blame for what had happened. She was filled with so many unanswerable questions that dangled around her like live wires. And then there was the inescapable guilt. "I didn't protect my baby and that was my job," Shari told me. The womb should be the safest place in the world for a baby to be. It is supposed to be a place of protection and nourishment, and Shari felt that she hadn't sheltered her baby properly from harm.

Most of all, Shari was overwhelmed by sadness and grief. She had felt so close to Daniel during all the months of her pregnancy. She experienced him as a remarkably active and energetic baby boy. But now she would never get to know him. She missed him so much, and she would never have the privilege of watching him grow and develop.

Soon Shari and Michael joined a support group for parents of stillborn infants. The mothers talked to one another daily on the phone. They expressed their anger and sadness and guilt. Shari found a sense of purpose in being able to offer help to other women who were just now going through the horror she had already endured. The bonds between the women were formed almost instantly. It's very rare to make that kind of connection with people in life, but the tragedy they had in common brought them into intense closeness. It was their similar experience that made them able to also laugh about what had happened to them. Only among themselves could they make jokes, jokes that would sound horrifying to anyone who had never lost a child, but that helped these grieving mothers release their agony. Together they could laugh about the stupid things some nurses had done in the hospital, the ridiculous comments some friends had made, and the strange way in which they often found themselves comforting the very people who should have been offering them comfort. Their laughter came from a knowledge of shared sorrow and shared love.

Another thing these mothers had in common was a desire to keep the memories of their deceased babies alive. When faced with the question "How many children do you have?" Shari answers differently depending upon her mood and whether or not she wants to get into a long conversation with a given stranger. But when the moment is right, she responds, "I am the mother of three children: Noah, Daniel, who died just before he was born, and Hillary [the daughter Shari gave birth to sixteen months after Daniel's death]."

One day an old friend of Shari's named Suzy came to see her. They had been teammates on their college gymnastics team. As they were lying on her bed and talking about Daniel's birth and death, Suzy said, "Shari, this doesn't happen to us." Shari knew just what her friend meant. Shari had always felt like one of the lucky ones. Everything she had ever done in life she had done well. She was always a leader and a good student, had always been offered wonderful opportunities. She was an accomplished athlete with a master's degree from Harvard, a prestigious job, a great marriage, a wonderful child, close friends. And now this. She had always felt blessed, protected, charmed. But reality had come crashing down on her and now she had to begin the long and difficult process of redefining herself. She had to look at herself in the mirror and say, "I'm no longer one of the untouchables."

All of us who have endured a tragedy know this feeling. One minute we define ourselves as completely "normal," protected and safe. The next minute we become the target of life's cruel blow. We are now the victims, the bereaved, the abused, the ill, the injured, the unemployed. Now we can no longer look upon suffering as the fate of those poor unfortunate souls out there. Now it is *our* inheritance. And now people are beginning to speak about us with the strange combination of pity and relief that we never dreamed would come our way. Pity, because they cannot feel our pain. Relief, because they are secretly glad that it is we who have been singled out for agony and not them.

It is so hard to believe that your entire world can change so dramatically overnight. Nothing is as it was. Lifelong friends don't seem to know what to say. Business acquaintances try to make believe that nothing has happened. Your relationship with God is thrown into turmoil. Your concept of self is shattered.

All of us who have endured pain must, at some point, go through a trying process of redefinition. We may want to continue pretending that nothing has changed, but when we try to deny or erase the blow we have suffered, it ends up becoming a source of secrecy and shame, of humiliation and disgrace. We should never be embarrassed by our misfortune. Having been hurt by life is not a sign of weakness; it can be a source of enormous strength, even heroic strength. We have to be willing to look at ourselves and say: "I am a person whose marriage failed." "I am an alcoholic." "I am an orphan." "I am a widow." Or, as Shari puts it, "I am the mother of a dead child." Then we have to be willing to embrace the full force of these words. These words do not define who we are—they define *part* of who we are. But it is a part we must face and acknowledge.

It's very hard to accept this new self-definition, to identify ourselves as among the wounded. However, when we finally gather up the courage to see ourselves as the vulnerable mortals that we indeed are, we may find that this new identity is far less frightening than we had imagined. It's much easier to live with the truth than it is to live with a lie. The truth is that the people who walk around feeling invulnerable are the ones who are fooling themselves. Of course, it is terrifying to learn that we are helpless to prevent bad things from happening to us. But the wisdom we gain from our suffering can enable us to appreciate life in a way we have never before known. When experience has taught us that our lives can be shattered in an instant, we learn to treat each day with reverence. We can no longer take joyous moments for granted as we used to; we appreciate them now as precious gifts. When we meet someone who needs our help, the pity we would have shown is replaced with empathy. Distance is replaced with understanding, callousness with love. Suddenly we know exactly how to offer help. We are no longer tongue-tied or uncomfortable. We can look a person who is in agony right in the eye and say, "I know, I've been there."

Tragedy has changed Shari's relationship with God. "I feel closer to God now because I never thought much about God until Daniel's death," she explained. Now, for the first time in her life, religion is a huge source of comfort and joy.

The name Daniel means "God has judged me." Shari certainly does not understand God's justice, but she believes, in the depths of her being, that there was a purpose and a meaning in Daniel's life and death. Although his death has left her feeling cheated, crushed, and angry, she is nevertheless grateful for the brief time she was privileged to carry his sacred life within her.

A Prayer

I am hurting, God. I feel lost, helpless, and alone. My tragedy seems so senseless. Help me, God, to embrace what I cannot understand, to find meaning in my suffering. Remind me that though I am powerless to choose my fate, I hold the power to choose a response to my fate. May I never be defeated. May I never grow bitter. May my sorrow lead me to strength, to wisdom, to compassion, and to You.

Amen.

CHAPTER SEVENTEEN

Conquering Envy

AFTER OVERCOMING our denial and redefining ourselves, we must then attempt to conquer the most insidious emotion that our misfortunes may have produced within us: envy.

It's easy and natural to feel envious when you are in pain and your friends are not. It's difficult not to be bitter when you are suffering from a serious illness, wondering whether you will live or die, and your friends are healthy, unburdened by such worries. When your business is failing and you're struggling just to make ends meet, it's hard to like your friends who are succeeding. When you have spent years all alone praying that you will find love, marriage, and babies and your friends are happily married with a brood of children, it's almost impossible to wish them well. The same is true when you have lost a loved one and your friends have never experienced that level of grief and loss.

When I was in high school, after my father's death, my friend Susan invited me to sleep over at her house on a Friday night. We played piano, sang, and gossiped for hours. Her mother was cooking the Sabbath dinner, and the sumptuous smell of roast chicken and onions filled the air. Then her father arrived, and we were all summoned to the dinner table. I had never met her father before. He was short and bald, and he reminded me of my father. We lit the Sabbath candles and stood up as Susan's dad recited the blessing over the wine. I had forgotten what it felt like to have a father's presence at the dinner table. At my home, the responsibility of presiding over all the Sabbath blessings had fallen on me. Afterward Susan's father hugged her, kissed her lovingly on top of her head, and said, "Good Shabbas to you, my little angel." I could see that Susan was embarrassed. In my presence she wanted to seem adult and mature, yet her father was treating her like a little girl. She rolled her eyes at me, the way teenagers do, as if to say, "I'm so above this childishness." But I would have given anything to have my father's hug and kiss once more. At that moment my heart was filled with envy. My eyes started to fill up with tears, but I bit my bottom lip until the hurt passed.

I have known many people who have let jealousies destroy them, who have isolated themselves, ruined friendships, and broken off relationships with loved ones because they simply couldn't bear to be around anyone who was happy. It makes sense. When we are in pain, happy people seem shallow, frivolous, superficial. We're spending our days thinking about ultimate issues, they're worrying about what floor tiles to put in their kitchen. Their concerns seem so foolish, so selfish, and blind. But wouldn't we give anything to have such a simple worry again? Is there no way to move beyond envy?

WHEN I WAS first dating Rob, the man to whom I am now married, he couldn't wait for me to meet Lloyd, his best friend and first cousin. I had heard stories about the vacations they had taken together, about adventures and mouthwatering dinners and old girlfriends. So you can imagine that I was more than a little nervous the first time Lloyd came down from San Francisco to visit. I was anxious for the two of us to hit it off. You know how awful it is when your best friend and your girlfriend don't get along. But from the moment I met Lloyd, I understood why Rob loved him so much. He was charismatic, funny, and easy. He didn't make me feel as though I was being judged or rated, and within minutes the two of us realized how much we had in common. We spent an entire afternoon walking along the beach, singing every lyric to every Beatles song we could think of. We sang the second side of *Abbey Road* without a break. We made a picnic and spoke about relationships and about God. Later we played guitar, then Lloyd opened up his sketchbook and showed me some of his remarkable portraits of friends, sunsets, and flowers. Lloyd was also strikingly handsome, with dark olive skin and gray-green eyes and a penetrating stare. His body was lean and muscular, graceful and agile. He was a guitarist, a composer, a singer, and a painter. In short, he was the last person you'd want to introduce to your new girlfriend. That night the three of us sat on the couch in sweatpants munching on popcorn and telling stories.

About a month before our wedding, Lloyd came down to visit. He was telling us a story about his latest girlfriend when he complained about a strange twitch in his left arm. I told him he should go see a doctor. He said, "It's probably nothing, just a pinched nerve or something." The week before our wedding Lloyd was diagnosed with amyotrophic lateral sclerosis, Lou Gehrig's disease, a disease that progressively paralyzes all the muscles in your body until you die.

At first we all thought there must be some mistake. The test results had to be wrong. It felt as if some strange joke were being played. But over time the shock gave way to the brutal realization that Lloyd was slowly losing his strength. Initially, the disease just affected his left arm. That in itself was a huge blow, since Lloyd was left-handed. Soon he couldn't draw anymore, play the guitar, or even sign his name. But, determined not to give in, Lloyd started to draw with his right arm. He started taking meditation classes and all sorts of holistic medicines. He read countless books about healing. Despite all that, he soon began losing his strength in his right arm, then in his legs.

During this time Lloyd was surrounded with good friends who did all they could for him. I have never seen a person with so many people willing to do so much. But soon Lloyd needed more attention than his friends could possibly give. He needed round-the-clock care.

On our last visit to Berkeley, I was seven or eight months pregnant. It was shocking to see how quickly Lloyd's disease had progressed. He could barely walk; his arms were virtually useless; he was thin and pale and could no longer shave himself. But his spirits were surprisingly high. We went out to dinner at a restaurant where Lloyd asked me if I believed in reincarnation. I told him that I did, that it was a very old Jewish mystical belief. We spoke about the soul and about God and eternity. He told me that he was sure there must be some existence beyond this tangible world, that losing his body had heightened his awareness of his soul. We took a long car ride, then stopped to watch the sun set over the water. We tried to sing some old Simon and Garfunkel songs, but Lloyd had lost the strength in the muscles that control breathing. All that came out was a breathy whisper. When we got back to his apartment, I remember watching him shuffle his feet to get from the table to the kitchen and feeling so guilty that I was carrying life in my belly. It was hard to deal with the fact that Rob and I were preparing for joy while Lloyd was slowly preparing to die. Each day brought new humiliation for him, new weakness and new concessions. His gifts, all the talents God had given him, existed now only in his mind. His once dashing physique was now a frail mass of bones. Yet his eyes still shone with astonishing humor. He seemed to be laughing at his own predicament, as if this crazy thing were happening not to him but to someone else.

One day Lloyd shared the following experience with me. He said that he'd had a remarkable vision. He was sitting in a chair and saw his healthy body leave his crippled body and walk away into the daylight. He asked me if I believed it was possible to have a vision. I said I was sure that it was. He told me that his vision was both sad and comforting at the same time. In one sense, it represented a loss: he had lost his healthy self. But in another sense it represented a freedom: his healthy self was free, it was roaming the earth taking in all the beauty of the world.

In July I gave birth to a beautiful baby boy, and in August Rob began trying to persuade Lloyd to move down to Los Angeles. At first Lloyd resisted the idea. He didn't know where he would live or how he would adjust. He had fought too hard for his independence to move back into his parents' home, he said. The very next day our neighbor told us she was moving out. Rob and I looked at each other, and we both had the same thought: this could be perfect for Lloyd. He'd be right beside us. We could visit him, we could have fun times, and he wouldn't have to worry about adjusting to some strange neighborhood.

And we simultaneously had another thought: this was going to be horrible—horrible, painful, and ugly. After a short period of deliberation, we agreed. And when our son was three months old, Lloyd came to live beside us. It was a period of adjustment but also of great exhilaration. It was nice to have him there, nice knowing that we could help his parents, sister, and attendants care for him. We would take long walks on the beach, Rob pushing Lloyd's wheelchair while I pushed our son Adi's stroller. People stared, children pointed. We rented movies and spent many a night watching great films.

The parallels between Lloyd and Adi were striking and poignant. Neither could speak, neither could walk. They both had to be hand-fed. Adi drank with a bottle, Lloyd with a straw. They both made their desires known through eye movements and gestures. They both had to be read to. They were two human beings at opposite ends of life's cycle, each locked in his respective helplessness. As time passed, Adi began to develop skills and strengths while Lloyd's skills and strengths continued to wane. There we were, separated by just one thin wall and by drastically different fates. But I never, not once, felt that Lloyd had any jealousy or anger toward us. He seemed to sincerely derive joy from our joy.

There was a daily parade of women who came through Lloyd's apartment. Whenever I asked who a certain woman was, she'd explain, "Oh, I'm Lloyd's old girlfriend." I've never met a person with as many girlfriends as Lloyd. All he had to do was look at a woman and immediately she'd fall under his spell. Even toward the end. A woman fell madly in love with Lloyd in the last months of his life when not only could he barely move, he could hardly communicate at all. His eyes were the only things left that worked. Yet she lived with him, slept in his room, took care of him.

There are times in life when, faced with a crisis, we find that we have strengths we never knew we had before. There are times when we surprise ourselves and rise to an occasion in ways we never would have expected. There are also times in life when trying situations actually make us aware of our weaknesses, of our fears and faults. Day after day with Lloyd living next door, I learned how difficult it was for me to face life's ugliness. I know that sounds unbelievable coming from a rabbi who, on a daily basis, has to deal with sickness, death, hospitals, final confessions, and funerals. But it's one thing to have to summon up the will to confront death on specific occasions; it's another to have to live with it day to day, minute to minute. I found myself in an internal battle whenever I walked up the steps to our apartment: "Should I go home and see my son, or should I go in and see Lloyd? Shall I embrace life, or shall I face down death?" I had to muster every ounce of my will even to set foot in Lloyd's apartment. Days would pass when I wouldn't stop by. There were always excuses: "I'm so busy. I'm in such a hurry. The baby's crying." But I am sure Lloyd heard every one of my footsteps. He knew each time I left home and each time I returned. And when I finally did gather up the courage to go next door, after being absent for several days, I always expected to receive a thrashing. I waited for Lloyd to look at me with hate-filled eyes or a resentful gaze that said, "And where have *you* been lately?"

But he never ever did any such thing. Instead, he'd look at me with caring eyes that said, "It's so good to see you," then use his letter board to tell some funny story. He had all the reason in the world to be spiteful toward me, but he never, not once, made me feel guilty. All he ever made me feel was welcome.

Of the two of us, Lloyd was the one who deserved compassion, but strangely enough he had the rare ability to *offer* compassion. With his eyes Lloyd seemed to be saying, "I know this isn't a pleasant place to be. I don't blame you for not coming more often. Believe me, I don't want to be here, either."

What made Lloyd become compassionate rather than envious or embittered? The most obvious answer is that he was acutely aware of just how little time he had left on this earth. He, more than most of us, understood how precious every day of his life was. Why waste it in resentment?

But there was another force that propelled this extraordinary man. I believe it had to do with his yearning to be free. When we bear a grudge, we generally assume that *we* are the ones who are empowered. We feel indignant and superior, replaying in our minds the various ways a given person has wronged us. But resentment is actually a cage. It is a prison that prevents us from repairing hurts or sustaining lifelong friendships. One prison was enough for Lloyd. His body had been taken hostage by a cruel and unforgiving disease, leaving him conquered and ravaged. He could no longer speak, walk, or move even a single limb. But his mind and his heart were free, unfettered. And he was determined to *keep* them free.

.   .   .

IT WAS A Thursday night and I was performing a naming ceremony for a beautiful little baby girl. When I returned home, Rob said, "It's the end." I started to feel queasy. Scared of facing death, I wasn't sure I wanted to go next door. But I went. Lloyd sat on a big reclining chair surrounded by family and friends. I took his hand and sat beside him on the floor. All our conversations about death and rebirth were now being lived out in these precious moments. As painful as this scene was, it was also quite beautiful. Lloyd was surrounded by love. His mother and his father were beside him, as they had been on the day of his birth. A holy glow shone forth from his face. Soon Lloyd slipped out of consciousness. His breaths grew ever more shallow. The vision he had once shared with me began to come alive before me. His gnarled and stiff hands suddenly became smooth and relaxed. I felt his healthy soul rise up and leave his tortured body behind. At last Lloyd was released from this cruel existence. He was finally free and at peace.

IN THE COURSE of his illness, Lloyd developed an uncanny ability. It was as if he could leave his body and enter yours. And from this new vantage point he was able to comprehend actions that otherwise might have hurt him. Another person might have been offended by people who stared at him in the street, or furious with friends who managed to disappear when the going got rough. But Lloyd seemed to see straight inside people's souls. He understood, he sympathized, he forgave.

We all need to banish the envy that embitters our lives. Left unchecked, it will destroy all our relationships and leave us isolated and angry. We must find the strength to take pleasure in other people's joys even when we are in pain. We must search for the wisdom to forgive people for not always being strong enough to face us in our misery. We must remember that our jealousies and resentments only add to our suffering. The longer we delay dealing with them, the longer we will remain imprisoned in our own pain.

We live our lives thinking that we have all the time in the world to change, all the time in the world to forgive or to ask for forgiveness. We say to ourselves, "I'm not emotionally ready to deal with this confrontation, but I'll get around to it." But we don't. Do we want to waste our time on this earth by bearing lifelong grudges against those we love? Do we want to waste it by not being a little more forgiving of those we are closest to? What does it take to be a little more accepting of people's flaws? Like Lloyd, each of us has the power and the strength to mend relationships with human beings and even with God. Like Lloyd, each of us has the power to move from envy to compassion. Only when we can gather the strength to exercise this power will we come to understand what returning to life really means.

A PRAYER

Soften my hardened heart, God. In my suffering I have grown callous and unforgiving. Secretly I've been wishing for my friends to fall. But this envy of mine is causing me to fall. Teach me, God, to cherish all that I am, all that I have, all that I have yet to offer. Help me to rejoice in the joy of others even when I am in pain; to take pleasure in their pleasure; to wish them nothing but blessings and peace.
Amen.

CHAPTER EIGHTEEN

Subduing Our Guilt

TO CONQUER our envy, we must learn how to love and forgive others. To subdue our guilt, we must learn how to love and forgive *ourselves*.

It is virtually impossible to experience tragedy without feeling guilt. "I should have done things differently." "I could have done more." "It's my fault this happened." These are the refrains that run through our minds when a tragedy strikes.

Sometimes our guilt is well founded. There are plenty of careless and irresponsible things we do that we *should* feel guilty about: things that bring pain to those we love; addictions that tear families apart; adultery that destroys trust; deceit, betrayal, cruelty, theft. We should feel guilty when we do something wrong. It is a healthy response, a sign of a conscience. People who feel no guilt frighten me, they don't seem human. Healthy guilt teaches us remorse, and it reminds us to behave differently in the future. But excessive guilt, even in those cases when we have done something wrong, is a misuse of our energy. We should be spending our time concentrating on improving ourselves, not on berating ourselves.

We often feel guilt when someone close to us dies before we have repaired our relationship with him or her. We blame ourselves for procrastinating, for not having had the emotional strength to say the words we needed to say, for having lacked the capacity to forgive when we still had the opportunity.

Once a mother brought her six-year-old son, Joey, into my office to talk to me. Joey was pale and shaking. I gave him a hug and asked him what was the matter. He told me that his friend Andy had died in a car accident. Joey and I had a long conversation about death, but I got the feeling that Joey had something very specific to get off his chest. Finally, he said to me, "When we were playing together last week, I kicked Andy on purpose." "And you feel bad about that now?" I asked. Joey started to cry, then he said, "Yes." I asked Joey what he would say to Andy if he were still alive. He answered, "I'd say, 'I'm sorry I kicked you.'" The minute Joey said those words, I could see that a spell had been broken. The little boy felt relieved. He couldn't apologize to Andy in person, but he could verbalize his regret and that seemed to lighten his load quite a bit.

Whenever congregants talk to me about the guilt they are feeling toward someone who has died, I recommend that they direct their apology to the deceased. One congregant of mine went to his father's grave to ask for forgiveness. Another wrote a long letter to her mother, telling her how sorry she was that she had taken her for granted. A man in his eighties spoke the words to his daughter that he had never been able to utter in her lifetime: "I love you."

The lesson we should learn from our feelings of regret is very simple: We should try with all our might to repair our relationships with those we love right now, every single day.

Ellen had always had a troubled relationship with her mother. Now her mother was dying of cancer; she was receiving terminal care in the hospital. Suddenly Ellen had an overwhelming need to tell her mother how sorry she was for all the pain she had caused her, but her mother was so heavily sedated that she just floated in and out of consciousness. Ellen asked her mother's doctor to turn off her morphine drip for a while so that they could talk. The doctor scolded her, telling her she was being selfish to put her mother through agony just so she could clear her guilty conscience. He was thinking of his patient's physical pain, which was no doubt intense. Nevertheless, Ellen persisted, and when her mother was alert she proceeded to pour her heart out to her. The two women shed tears, embraced, and bid each other farewell. That single hour of closeness between mother and daughter perhaps offered more pain relief than morphine could ever have provided.

But there are awful situations that we feel guilty about for no reason at all.

When Pat learned that he was dying of stomach cancer, he came to tell me that he was sure the cancer was his fault. Perhaps he should have eaten more healthfully or gotten more rest. Perhaps he shouldn't have been working so hard. Perhaps he shouldn't have sat so close to the color television set for all those years. Pat was so busy blaming himself that he forgot to be kind to himself. I asked him how he would respond if he learned that a close friend of his had been diagnosed with cancer. Would he start accusing him of wrongdoing? Would he tell his friend that he was to blame for his illness? Of course not. He would offer help and compassion. Pat began to see my point, and did eventually embrace the idea that he hadn't caused his cancer. It was a realization that gave him the courage to begin to confront his impending death.

Lori is quite beautiful, close to six feet tall, with long blond hair and deep green eyes. One day she came to see me in tears and told me that she had been in a two-year relationship with a man she loved deeply, named Tod. She had taken it for granted that they would eventually be married. But Tod had come home the night before and announced that the relationship was over. He wanted out. Lori was in shock. There had been no warning signs that a breakup was coming. She kept asking him what the problem was. Couldn't they work things out? Couldn't they go to therapy? Had she done something to make him angry or hurt him? But he denied that his decision had anything to do with

her. He told her that he simply needed space. And not temporary space, but *permanent* space. Lori started to tell me more,
but began sobbing uncontrollably. She kept trying to get out the
words but all that emerged was a series of gasps. I held her
hand, gave her a box of tissues, and waited. After a few minutes
she took some deep breaths and said, "Seven years ago I accidentally gave a boyfriend of mine a sexually transmitted disease.
I'm sure that's why this is happening to me now. I think God's
punishing me for that sin I committed seven years ago." I told
Lori how sorry I was that her relationship with Tod was over. I
added that I didn't believe that her past transgression had anything to do with her present troubles. But she was adamant. She
knew *she* was to blame for the situation in her past, and she was
sure that every bad thing that had come her way ever since that
time was a punishment for that single sin.

I knew how she felt. When I was in the ninth grade, a classmate of mine lost her mother. I felt terribly sorry for her, but
I also couldn't help noticing that the timing of her mother's
death couldn't have been better. It was during finals week, so
my friend was excused from all her exams; the teachers felt so
bad for her that they just gave her high grades out of sympathy.
I thought to myself, "What a great deal. Wouldn't that be nice
if one of my parents died during finals?" Exactly one year later
my father was killed during finals week. I too was excused
from all my exams. I too received undeservedly high grades
from my teachers. And I was certain that I had caused my
father's death. I had wished it, after all. What I wouldn't have
given at that moment to be able to take Madame Rosen's ridiculous French final.

Judaism's traditional response to all the horrible events that
befell the Jews throughout their history was: God is punishing
us for our sins. It was because of the people's sins that the Temple in Jerusalem, their central place of worship, was destroyed.
It was because of the people's sins that they were exiled from

their land. "We must have brought this upon ourselves" is the common refrain in so many Jewish sacred texts.

How can we believe in a God who slaughters innocent children just because their parents have sinned? Or a God who punishes us by hurting the innocent people we love? How can we believe in a God who would destroy our lives for the sake of a minor infraction? To believe in such a God is not only an insult to us, it's an insult to God as well. We don't deserve the awful fate that has befallen us. God is not a sadist up in the sky looking for some feeble excuse to cause us pain.

Isn't there some way for us to stop punishing ourselves for every horrible thing that happens to us? I believe that many of us hold on to our guilt because in some strange way it helps us to survive, to retain our sanity in the face of life's insanity. Guilt helps us because it creates order out of chaos. It gives us a way to retain the belief that the tragedy that has befallen us is not just haphazard, is not just senseless. It has a cause. Our guilt tells us that *we* are the cause. It allows us to feel powerful in the face of a tragedy that leaves us feeling helpless and small. So powerful, in fact, that we are willing to hold our very selves responsible for events that were clearly out of our control.

Guilt helps us to restore meaning to our lives in the wake of tragedy. The world no longer seems unpredictable, God no longer seems capricious. But this kind of guilt comes at a huge price. How long can we continue persecuting ourselves for circumstances we didn't cause? Admittedly, life without groundless guilt is frightening—terrifying, in fact. It means that our existence is unpredictable, that horrible things can happen to us at any time for no reason at all, that God is not our punishing parent. But life without groundless guilt is also liberating. Finally, we can stop torturing ourselves and start forgiving ourselves for not being everything we fantasize we could be. We can stop carrying a heavy heart into every new situation and break the never-ending cycle of suffering that began the moment our tragedy struck. We can, at last, allow ourselves to feel joy once more, to believe that we deserve to have fun once more. Finally, we can stop fearing God and start approaching God in love, in protest, in sadness, in longing, in joy.

Of course, it's easy to talk about eradicating groundless guilt and much more difficult to actually achieve it. The first step is to simply acknowledge the irrationality of most guilt feelings.

The next step is to think about God, who gave you this life so that you might live it in all its glory. There is a teaching in the Jerusalem Talmud that we will be held accountable on Judgment Day for all the permissible pleasures in this world which we failed to partake of. Remember that God does not want you to continue to inflict senseless torture on yourself. Return to the phrase "Let me not die while I am still alive." Try to repeat these words over and over again until they take root in your very being. You may not be able to free yourself of all guilt, but you may be able to achieve what your heart has been longing for: peace.

A Prayer

I've been blaming myself, God, for the tragedy that has befallen me. The thoughts keep running through my mind like a tune I can't seem to shake: "I could have done more." "I should have done more." But none of this self-loathing can erase the past. Teach me, God, to believe that I don't deserve to be punished forever. Help me to forgive and to love myself despite my weakness. Show me Your love, this day and always.
Amen.

CHAPTER NINETEEN

Learning to Stop Flinching

A PERSISTENT STRUGGLE we must face when we have been hurt by life is the struggle to teach our hearts to remain open. The desire to protect ourselves from future pain is natural. It makes so much sense. Why would anyone ever want to feel pain like that again? But of course, if we never open ourselves up to the possibility of getting hurt, we become our own tormentors. We rob ourselves of all the love and the enjoyment that we could be experiencing.

There are so many different ways in which we allow the tragedies of our past to destroy our present. Some people react to every new situation by being defensive. Others run away from commitment or from situations that might leave them feeling open and vulnerable. Others shut down their emotional lives, cutting themselves off from their feelings. Still others find themselves always trying to please. They worry so much about being abandoned or mistreated that they turn themselves into human Gumby dolls, bending and stretching in every direction to accommodate the whims of whomever they are with.

Over my years in the pulpit, I got pretty good at detecting people who lived life expecting others to hurt them. They are the ones who take every neutral event and personalize it as a deliberate slight. They allow everything in the present to be colored, or discolored, by some painful event in the past.

One day a thin woman in her late fifties with dark hair and dark eyes came to see me in my study. She sat down and said, "Rabbi, I'm going to get right to the point. When you came around to greet the congregation during services last week, you shook everybody's hand but mine. Do you have something against me? Are you purposely trying to ignore me? You've really hurt my feelings." I was completely in shock. I couldn't believe what I was hearing. Did this woman actually think that I knew whose hand I had shaken? Didn't she realize that there were so many hands and that I just shook as many as I could? I was also a bit peeved by her very visible anger—until it occurred to me that to feel this strongly about a missed handshake, this woman must have been horribly mistreated or ignored by someone in her life. When I later learned that her childhood was filled with neglect, her reaction to a missed handshake began to make sense to me. Her painful childhood experiences trained her to fear even the slightest hint of rejection.

Of course, there is no way to erase this woman's past. She will carry it with her forever. But I wish she could learn to see that the present is not simply a replaying of the past. By reacting defensively all the time, by relating to everything in her present as if it were directly connected to her past, she actually *created* her own isolation. She *caused* people to avoid her. After all, who wants to befriend a person who is always accusing you of hurting them?

When we suffer a blow, it's completely natural to experience feelings of rage and hopelessness, distrust and despair. But eventually, these feelings should subside. We have to work to *make* them subside. To carry such emotions with us forever is self-defeating. They will prevent us from seeing that our lives are not, in fact, cursed. They will blind us from noticing all the new blessings that surround us each and every day.

In the Bible, in the Book of Leviticus, God reveals to the

Children of Israel that the greatest torment that will befall them will be a suffering that has no basis in reality:

". . . And the sound of a shaken leaf shall chase them; and they shall flee, as fleeing from a sword; and they shall fall when none pursues."

It is a terrible curse, made so by the fact that it comes from nowhere but our own hearts. The blows we endure in our lives usually come from the outside. But the worst torture is the one we inflict upon ourselves. Each and every one of us knows this curse all too well. Sooner or later we all find ourselves reacting not to the present event before us but to some old hurt, some distant wound. We are all aware of the pieces of ourselves that we have let die because of some pain that took place in the past. Perhaps we have lost our ability to trust, or to love, or to believe that our lives can and will get better. That's what happens when the past invades and destroys the present.

It is normal to flinch in reaction to something that reminds us of a past pain. That reaction is built into our nature. In fact, that flinch can be lifesaving. We should know to pull our hands away from a fire or to keep our distance from the class bully. But if you've ever tried to pet a dog that is hand-shy you know what it means to see a creature that is permanently locked inside its abusive past. Somehow this lifesaving instinct can take over and cause us to flinch at perfectly benign experiences. "After you've been bitten by a snake," goes a Yiddish proverb, "you're afraid even of a piece of rope."

There is a choice to make and we all must make it. We can allow the past to paralyze us, to prevent us from facing the future and all its wonderful potential, or we can struggle to remain open to embrace all the gifts that God bestows upon us each day.

. . .

ON THE DAY my son was born, Rob and I looked at him in utter amazement. Before us lay a totally innocent little being who knew nothing of the ugliness of this world. He had no fears, no baggage from the past. As we watched him take in his surroundings, we found it difficult to even think of a name for him. At that moment he was pure potential. He could be anyone.

Then, a week later, the day of his bris arrived, a bittersweet ritual if ever there was one. We agonized about the painful ritual we were about to subject him to. How could we willingly and intentionally cause him pain?

I held him close that morning. Looking into his achingly innocent eyes, I tried to explain. I told him in my heart about the gift of history, about the beauty of his religion and the precious legacy that he was about to receive. I also told him about the hatred and the prejudice that are also the inheritance of his people. I explained how much I wanted to shelter him from pain and suffering, how I never wanted him to know fear. And then I acknowledged to myself that I could never fully save him from experiencing the ugliness of this world. We all must eventually face it. But I prayed that he would somehow find the ability to remain open in the face of life's pain; that he would not allow his heart to grow callused and hard. I prayed that no matter what hurts came his way, he would find the strength not to flinch at the sound of a shaken leaf.

This prayer of mine is no fantasy. I believe it can be achieved. I have known people who have fought fearlessly to remain open in the face of tragedy. If we hope to live our lives fully, we must achieve it. We can all learn to recapture our innocence no matter what form of hell we have lived through.

LOUIS is a distinguished-looking man with a thick head of graying hair, a debonair mustache, and an accent that speaks of faraway places and times. Louis has a wonderful wife, Dina, and the joy of their lives is their grandchildren. I have known Louis for nine years. He is one of the dependable ones: he comes to services every Friday night and every Saturday morning. That is, whenever he's in the country. Louis and Dina travel more often than just about anyone I have ever met, and for months at a time.

I've always been struck by Louis's eyes. They are the eyes of a child: curious and naive, soft and loving. But what stands out most of all about Louis is his love of children. Anytime a child is born in our community, Louis becomes its honorary grandfather. A baby will cry in the middle of the service and Louis will reach over, take the child in his arms, and amuse it in no time at all. Believe me, Louis has saved me from many an embarrassing moment. So often there would be a child making a racket during one of my sermons and people would start complaining, "How can a parent let their kid make so much noise during the rabbi's sermon? How rude!" And then Louis would scoop my son into his arms and quiet him down.

The first glimpse I had into Louis's painful past took place when he shared with me the following story. Over the past five decades Louis has been making a strange pilgrimage. Not to Mecca or Jerusalem, but to a place called Seeshaupt, Germany. He's gone there dozens of times, year after year, snapping hundreds upon hundreds of pictures of a small unremarkable train station, each time leaving without ever telling anyone why. On his last trip to Seeshaupt, Louis, as usual, stood in front of the train station with his wife Dina, shooting scores of photos. After hours of standing in the same spot, Dina started to get annoyed with him. "You've taken enough pictures already," she said. "Let's go." But Louis said that he wanted to wait until a freight train passed by. So they waited and waited, hoping that such a train would eventually come. Hours passed. Dina finally got impatient enough to say, "This doesn't make any sense. There must be an office inside this station. Why don't we just ask for a schedule?" So they went inside and he asked, "When will the next freight train be going through here?" The man at the window replied, "Sir, there hasn't been a freight train through here in forty-nine years. But forty-nine years ago, on this very day, such a train did come through here. A cattle train, filled with three thousand Jews from the camps. The American soldiers opened the doors and the villagers looked inside and saw that the cars were filled with corpses."

Louis turned to the clerk and said, "I know. You're looking at one of those corpses."

I've never forgotten those words, nor the mixture of pain and irony in Louis's youthful eyes. On one sunny March afternoon I went to Louis's apartment to ask him to share with me his memories of those years of pain and torment.

Louis grew up in a small village in the south of Hungary. The Jewish population numbered four hundred and fifteen, an observant and very close community. At the age of three, boys began going to cheder, religious school, to study Torah. The synagogue not only stood at the center of their town, it served as the center of their lives. The Sabbath stood as the focal point of their week. Life was good, dominated by community, family, and God, and with enough food to stretch a small fish into a feast. Was there anything lacking? Electricity, running water, a toilet, perhaps, but who knew to desire such things?

In 1944 the German army marched into Hungary. A series of laws had already been passed prohibiting Jews from eating kosher meat, owning land, and taking part in commerce. Louis's father was barred from selling dry goods at the local market. Louis was studying as an apprentice to an electrician, but the Nazis closed his school and deported his wise and kind mentor, Mr. Engelman, to a labor camp, where he was never heard from again. All Jews were forced to wear the yellow star. Louis's father, along with all other men ages eighteen to forty-eight, was ordered to report to his army unit. Louis accompanied his father to the train station. They hugged but didn't say goodbye. People were so busy loading the train that there was no time for discussion. At that moment Louis never imagined that this would be the last time he would ever see his father's sweet face.

Fourteen days later, all the people remaining in Louis's village were told that they were being evicted from their homes and that they could take with them only one piece of baggage. Without the men they were now three hundred souls: the elderly, women, and children, crammed together and forced to live in a horse stable.

The very next morning the young boys were called to report to work. Their job: to remove the contents of the homes of all the Jews. Led by a police officer, they went from house to house collecting their own furniture, their beds and tables and cherished possessions. Louis was one of those boys. He had to clear out his own house and the houses of all his neighbors, including the home of his beloved rabbi, with all its precious scholarly books. The boys brought all the furniture and belongings to the synagogue, where everything was piled high, until the village was officially deemed "Jew-free."

Six weeks later Louis and his fellow villagers were shipped to a regional ghetto. The conditions were appalling; there was filth, hunger, and overcrowding. But bad as things were, they were about to get dramatically worse. Soon they were pushed into the now infamous cattle cars. Ninety people huddled together in one small car; babies were crying, the elderly were hunched and groaning in the dark. They traveled in tension and confusion, fear and hunger, in complete panic, for days. Then, suddenly, the doors opened, light poured in, ferocious dogs barked at them, men in SS uniforms yelled, *"Raus! Raus!* Out! Out!"* It all happened like a whirlwind. Within seconds they were all out of the train. Before them stood an impeccably dressed man with a monocle. He didn't say a word, just held a baton in his hand and, as if he were conducting an orchestra, looked at each person and pointed either to the right or to the left. As he pointed, each person was herded in the direction indicated. The conductor was Dr. Josef Mengele. The train station was Auschwitz.

Just then Louis's mother saw a young woman struggling to quiet her crying baby. Louis's mother leaned over, took the child in her arms, and attempted to soothe it. Because of that child in her arms, Louis's mother was sent to the left. Louis was sent to the right. Again, there was no time for goodbyes. They just assumed they'd meet up later.

Louis was sent through "disinfection," where his head was shaved and his clothes taken away, replaced with a prison uniform. Along with eleven hundred other boys, he received no food or water and was forced to sleep on a concrete floor. Packed in like sardines, these eleven hundred boys were placed in lines of a hundred or so, each boy sitting between the spread legs of the boy in front of him. That is how they slept, in a room that could fit no more than fifty beds. The conditions were unspeakable, the hunger unbearable.

The next morning Louis and several friends saw a kapo, a prisoner appointed by the Nazis to oversee his fellow prisoners. The kapo had obviously been in Auschwitz for some time. They asked him, "Where are the mamas? When can we see our mamas?" And this callous Jewish kapo smiled, pointed to the smokestacks above the crematoria, and said, "You want to see your mamas? You can see them. *There* are your mamas. Right there!"

There was no time for grieving or mourning. In the face of this horrifying knowledge, in the face of hunger and torture, the only thought was: "How am I going to stay alive?"

Soon Louis was sent with a group of boys and men to a labor camp near a city called Mühldorf in Bavaria. Only because he had some background as an electrician was he spared the intense labor of his fellow inmates, who carried hundred-pound bags of cement on their backs until they died of exhaustion or were shot on the spot.

Louis spent the remainder of the war in Mühldorf until April 25, 1945, when the Nazis decided to clear the camp and dispose of all the Jews so that the Allies would not discover what had taken place there. Once again he was packed into a cattle car without food or water. Overhead the Allied bombs could be heard. The train itself came under attack more than once. Then, on the fifth day, the train stopped. Through the cracks, Louis saw Nazi guards tear off their uniforms, throw their weapons down, and run away into the woods. The doors of the train opened onto a small German town called Seeshaupt. It was a beautiful spring morning. The fruit trees were in full bloom. And then, miraculously, American GIs popped out of a large tank, smiling and offering them food.

Louis is what some would call a Holocaust survivor, but I have always disliked that word. To me it implies that someone is barely living. You ask a person how they're doing and they sigh and reply, "All right, I guess, I'm surviving." But Louis is not surviving, he is *living*. He is *thriving*. Yes, Louis found freedom on that April day in 1945, but somehow he found much more than freedom. Louis found life, too. Ever since then he has celebrated life, rejoiced in his blessings, and has never been cynical about human nature.

It certainly has not been easy for Louis. It can never be easy for someone who was one of only nine people to survive Auschwitz out of the four hundred and fifteen people in his village who were sent there. To this day he is hounded by images of the fallen. The haunting face of the rabbi's martyred son as he was being led to his death appears to Louis not only in dreams but when his eyes are wide open. The boy had been told that he was being taken to the hospital. But everyone knew what that meant: certain death. Nevertheless, the rabbi's son bid farewell to Louis with an expression of anguished optimism. "Yes, I'm going to the hospital," he said. Yet despite Louis's never-ending horror, he has consistently chosen life in the face of death, in the face of darkness and memory and nightmares and flashbacks. He has chosen life in the face of sadness and mourning.

On the fiftieth anniversary of his liberation, Louis was instrumental in erecting a monument in Seeshaupt commemorating the deliverance that had taken place there. At the dedication ceremony Louis chose to read these words from the Book of Psalms: "The cords of death encompassed me, the grave held me in its grip. . . . Be at ease once again, my soul, for the Lord has dealt kindly with you. God has delivered me from death, my eyes from tears, my feet from stumbling. I shall walk before the Lord in the land of the living."

Like Louis, we all have the potential to emerge from our suffering with an open heart. With a willingness to embrace the life that surrounds us no matter what we have endured in the past.

When I called Louis and asked him if I could have permission to tell his story, he replied, "I don't know what people can learn from me." But Louis was wrong. He has taught me and many others so much. He's shown me what it means to preserve the innocence of youth even when you've seen the hell that adults can create. He's taught me what it means to choose life even though you're haunted by death, to choose joy even though life is full of pain, to choose the future even though you are pursued by the past. That is what I believe we all want for ourselves and what God wants for each and every one of us.

Recently I sat beside Louis at Sabbath morning services. The rabbi who succeeded me was giving a sermon as I held my daughter Noa in my lap and tried to listen. Noa started to cry and I began to search for her bottle. But Louis leaned over and gently took her into his arms, the way his mother had done on that fateful day at Auschwitz. My daughter stretched out her hand, pulled on his mustache, and started to laugh. Then she nestled her head on his chest, smiled, and closed her eyes.

I pray that, like Louis, all of us can find a way to preserve the precious qualities that were God's gift to each and every one of us on the day of our birth: openness, innocence, gentleness, curiosity, and warmth. But in order to revive these gifts in ourselves, we first must begin to believe that we have the power to move beyond the suffering we have endured. Our hope that the future can and will be different from the past, our faith that we have the capacity to remake our very selves, will allow us to move forward without cynicism and without bitterness.

A Prayer

It is hard to trust when we have been hurt. It is hard to hope again when we have known tragedy. It is hard to stop flinching, to stop responding to past pains. It is hard to face the present with an open heart. Help me, God. Restore me. Revive in me all the optimism that I once had. Remind me of the person I used to be. Help me to return to life, to openness, and to You, my God.
Amen.

CHAPTER TWENTY

Returning to God

AFTER SEEKING HEALING for our minds and hearts, it is time to tend to our wounded souls.

Is there no way to rebuild our relationship with God after God has let us down? What are we to do when we have looked for signs of God but all we've seen is the *absence* of God? What are we to do when we've searched for God's presence, when we've prayed with all our hearts, but have received no response in return? Each of us who has suffered a tragedy knows what it feels like to have one's prayers go unanswered. Is it possible to recover our faith in a God who didn't answer our prayers? Who didn't heal the sick or alleviate suffering?

Rebecca came to synagogue with her father, Dennis, every single Saturday for Sabbath services. Her presence was felt the minute she walked through the door. I'd hear a thumping sound, and I'd look up to see Rebecca running down the aisle of the sanctuary. Then she'd make her way onto the pulpit, all the while clutching a shredded blanket. She'd say "Hi" to me, and then she was off to her next activity: riding her tricycle in circles around our small play-yard. Rebecca was a beautiful five-year-old child. She had wide blue-green eyes and curly golden-brown locks that dangled down her neck. To say that she was a leader would be an understatement. She was more like a force of nature. She was robust and determined and strong-willed.

When she wanted something, there was no way to ignore her. And she had quite a temper.

The members of our congregation had a special affection for Rebecca. She had been diagnosed with leukemia when she was just a toddler, and she had been in their prayers and hearts all through her months of chemotherapy. Now those awful days were just a shadow that hovered over Rebecca's past. She had emerged from her treatment with flying colors and was back to her old self, her newly grown head of hair bobbing up and down as she skipped gleefully through the synagogue each week.

I had only been Rebecca's rabbi for a few months when I got a call from Dennis. He was all choked up. Rebecca had relapsed. Their family's world had come crashing down. I came over in the early afternoon without knowing what I was going to say to Rebecca. I didn't know her well enough to take her in my arms. I wondered whether she would want me around at all. I walked through the door, and before I could open my mouth, this remarkable little girl pulled out a coloring book and some crayons and said, "Want to color with me?" I picked up a crayon and sat beside her. We colored. That was enough.

Then came the grueling months of chemotherapy. Every few weeks Rebecca was back in the hospital to receive intravenous drugs designed to destroy her cancer. The next time I came over, Rebecca's hair was starting to fall out again. She didn't seem to mind so much. She just turned to me and said, "My hair's falling out." But I could see that it was torturing her mother, Kathy. Kathy seemed heartbroken, pained to a depth that most human beings are never forced to reach.

On my following visit Rebecca was completely bald. She was in the hospital receiving her chemotherapy, but the baldness was the only outward sign that she was ill. When children have cancer, you expect them to look sickly, pale, thin, frail. But Rebecca always looked robust, strong, and playful. Full of life. It was hard to believe that she was suffering from such a serious condition. As soon as she could, after each treatment, she'd be back in the thick of things, prancing around and, of course, calling all the shots—until her next round of chemo.

Over time, as I continued to visit Rebecca, I got to know Kathy and Dennis better. And grew to be in awe of them. They were incredibly strong, absolutely unwavering in their love.

Seeing Rebecca in the hospital was heartbreaking. No child likes to be away from home. Even on vacation, children inevitably find themselves missing their beds and their toys and soon start begging, "Is it time to go home yet?" This was no vacation. Rebecca found herself in an alien, sterile environment where she was poked, prodded, and forced to endure all sorts of discomforts. But she handled it all like the toughest trouper. She'd bring her favorite books, her blanky, and her music tapes, and with her parents by her side, she'd make the best of it.

Rebecca loved music. She really had quite a musical ear and knew all the lyrics to every Disney video she had. Her favorite was *The Little Mermaid*. She loved Ariel and her world under the sea. I once sat with Rebecca watching the movie and was totally entranced, not by what I saw on the screen but by her ability to sing every word and every note of every song. In the movie Ariel, the mermaid, desperately longs to leave the stifling undersea world and enter the world of human beings. I imagined that Rebecca's attraction to the story had something to do with her identification with the mermaid. She too felt trapped and stifled—by her illness. Perhaps she dreamed of escaping to freedom under the sea, where she would be unleashed from the world of hospitals, needles, and doctors.

There was one occasion when the Make-a-Wish Foundation, the organization that enables sick children to live out a fantasy, got in touch with Rebecca and her family. Dennis told me that he hoped Rebecca would choose to meet someone really interesting like a great musician or a great actor. But when Rebecca was asked whom she'd like to meet, she said, "Minnie Mouse." There was something so beautifully naïve in her choice. She had no idea that Minnie Mouse was just an unknown person in a big old costume. Make-a-Wish made good on its promise. Rebecca was sent to Disneyland, where she met Minnie herself—and could not have been happier.

Rebecca was one of the most spiritual people I have ever known. She was only a child, but she had a purity of faith and a passion for learning that is rare even in devout adults. She loved going to synagogue and playing with all her friends there. But most of all she looked forward to standing on the pulpit at the end of the service and chanting along with the closing prayers. She was much younger than the other children in our Sunday school, but she wanted to go so badly that we included her in the class. The other children often whined about having to be in school on a Sunday morning, but Rebecca was always enthusiastic. She never wanted to miss a class, even when she was feeling weak. She soaked up the Hebrew language and the songs, the prayers and the Bible stories, like someone with an unquenchable thirst. And even when she had to miss class because of her treatments, Rebecca would return to school and catch up so quickly that she often ended up explaining things to the older children who had been there all along. Rebecca's favorite song was a prayer that a singer named Craig Taubman had set to pop music, "We are Your people and You are our God, Shema Yisrael Adonai Eloheynu Adonai Echad [Hear, O Israel, the Lord our God, the Lord is One]." I was once talking to Rebecca when this song came on, and she hopped out of her seat and started dancing and jumping around the living room in utter ecstasy. Was it just the lively music that got her dancing? I don't think so. I believe that the words reached out to her soul. The prayer kindled a rare kind of delight within her. Whenever she heard it, she seemed unfettered, released. The prayer became Rebecca's anthem.

The treatments were working. The cancer was going into remission. Things were looking up. After a few more months, Rebecca was through with chemotherapy, and her life began to return to normal. She was back at school, her hair was slowly growing, everyone was optimistic. She celebrated her sixth birthday with all her friends around her. It was a celebration of life, joy, and hope. Within the family, every milestone of Rebecca's took on enormous proportions. Kathy always wanted to make sure that whatever the occasion, the celebration was the best possible. She slaved to make everything perfect for her daughter, leaving no stone unturned. I remember how she stayed awake nights sewing a Little Mermaid costume for the hospital's Halloween party.

The only thing that Dennis and Kathy could not do for Rebecca was to heal her.

There is nothing more devastating to a parent than being unable to make things better for a child. When children fall, parents are always there to pick them up, kiss them, and say, "It's all better now." But Kathy and Dennis could not offer their daughter that comfort. They were helpless. Unfortunately, Rebecca's doctors were helpless, too. Not long after her sixth birthday, Rebecca was back in the hospital with a relapse.

This time the doctors told Dennis and Kathy that there was nothing they could do. No treatment would work. It was just a matter of time.

Rebecca's condition worsened by the hour. The next morning, around 7:00 a.m., Dennis called me and said, "It's time to come over." I raced over to the hospital, where Rebecca was in her bed, unconscious, with all her family members present. Her grandparents, cousins, uncles, aunts, and, of course, her parents. Rebecca was taking shallow breaths. This was the end. We watched and waited as her breaths grew ever weaker. But some-how she held on. All day long. At one point Dennis kneeled over her and whispered, "It's all right now, you can let go now. You don't have to fight anymore. It's OK to let go."

But Rebecca held on still. Later on in the afternoon, the nurse called me out of the room. Another family from our com-munity was phoning to let me know that they had just given birth to a beautiful baby boy. Filled with so many mixed emo-tions, I congratulated them and wished them joy, then resumed my place at the death vigil.

Inside the room, there was no sense of space or time. Min-utes seemed like hours, hours passed like seconds. As the day grew ever darker, fluid started to accumulate in Rebecca's lungs. When she breathed, you could hear the water inside of her. I imagined that Rebecca was finally entering Ariel's magical world under the sea.

I left the hospital room for a short while, and when I returned I learned that Rebecca had died. Dennis and Kathy were all alone in the room with their daughter's body. With Dennis, I performed the Jewish ritual of rending garments. I cut his shirt and he recited the blessing, "Blessed is the True Judge." Dennis wanted to perform ritual purification on Rebecca. I told him that it's done in the mortuary, but he wanted to cleanse her then and there. A nurse brought water. We carefully undressed Rebecca. Dennis poured water gently over her entire body, limb by limb, and over her hair, too. It was her final bath before her everlasting sleep. Now she would depart this world clean and pure. Kathy sat beside Rebecca and leaned over her. Her long blond hair fell over Rebecca's face, forming a private curtain. They were interlocked in a moment of everlasting intimacy. For as long as I live I will never forget that tragic sight of a mother leaning over her lifeless daughter, the soft strands of her hair covering her daughter's face like a shelter of love and peace. I don't know how Dennis and Kathy ever found the strength to leave Rebecca's side. But somehow they did.

The next time Dennis and Kathy saw her, Rebecca's small body lay quietly inside her casket, shrouded in white with her blanky by her side. The funeral was a day of unmitigated pain for Rebecca's family and our entire community. I barely made it through the eulogy. When Craig Taubman stood up with his guitar and sang Rebecca's Shema prayer, everyone present broke down. The days after that were days of intense communal outpouring. Our congregation gathered together at Dennis and Kathy's home to offer comfort and support and to pray each day, morning and night. You never know how much community means in your life until you need it. Dennis and Kathy were surrounded by love, it kept them afloat.

The months following Rebecca's death were brutal for her family and for our congregation. Every Sabbath our community would gather to pray—but somehow the prayers had lost their power. I suffered from the same despair. How could we be praying to a God who had allowed Rebecca to die? I thought that I had been through all those questions about God and the existence of evil long before. I thought that I had made a final and lasting peace with God. But Rebecca's death brought back all my questions, all my anger and disillusionment. But this time I wasn't a rebellious fifteen-year-old kid trying to carve out her own identity. This time I was the rabbi of a congregation that was looking to me for answers. How could I lead them in prayer when my heart was drowning in turmoil? I searched for courage and faith, but I couldn't seem to find any. Week after week, Sabbath services seemed to drone on without any sense of uplift.

Then I thought of Rebecca, and I drew my strength and my faith from her.

Most children believe that their parents possess a godlike omnipotence; that their parents can heal any ache and solve any problem. But too early in her life Rebecca knew better. She knew that her parents couldn't heal her, nor could they prevent her from being sick or from feeling pain. But this knowledge never stopped Rebecca from believing in her parents' power to help her. She knew how much her parents loved her. And that love gave her the strength to face her illness and even her death with courage and fearlessness.

Most adults believe that *God* possesses a godlike omnipotence; that God can heal any ache and solve any problem. But Rebecca knew better. Her faith was never about bargaining or pleading with God. She never expected anything from God except for the joy and the comfort that she received.

We adults didn't have Rebecca's faith. Her death caused our community to question God. We had prayed to God to heal Rebecca, but God did not save her. God could not prevent her from being sick or from feeling pain. For many of us, God's inaction called our faith into question. What good is a God who doesn't do anything? But then, over time, we began to remember Rebecca's unique relationship with God, and she became for us a model of pure faith. Rebecca showed our entire community how it is possible to feel healed even when we have not been cured. She showed us how to draw on God's power to find strength, compassion, and understanding. She showed us how it is possible to continue believing even when your faith has been shattered—even after your hero, your parent, or even your God, has been deflated. With a wisdom beyond her years, she showed us that we could be uplifted by God's comforting presence, even though God had not miraculously saved her life. Rebecca's pure faith gave our entire congregation the strength to carry on, even in the face of her death, with courage, with faith, and with hope.

A Prayer

When I was in trouble, I prayed to You, God, but You did not shield me from pain. Ever since then I've been unable to pray. Why should I plead for what You cannot or will not provide? Why should I talk when there is no one who will listen? It's embarrassing, humiliating, infuriating. And yet here I am talking to You once more. I no longer seek miracles from You, God; I ask only this: Be with me in my suffering.

Amen.

PART FOUR

The Turning Point

Over time, as we make our journey away from pain and toward life, something strange will happen to us. We may not even notice the gradual change. But one morning we will wake up and realize that we are feeling good, that we are actually taking pleasure in things, that small tasks don't seem as difficult and life doesn't seem as bleak. We may wonder how we ever got through the pain, but we will see that we are approaching the other end of the darkness. The light before us is visible and welcoming.

CHAPTER TWENTY-ONE

Stop

As THE DARKNESS LIFTS, don't let that moment pass without experiencing its full force. Take a walk, even if it's only around the block. Breathe deeply. Gaze at the trees, listen to the birds, look up at the sky, take in the beauty. Eat your favorite food. Savor every bite with a renewed appetite for living. Grate a lemon and smell its rind. Hug your family, thank your friends for standing by you when you were in pain. Ask forgiveness from those you alienated. Stand before a mirror and stare into your own eyes. See the hope that shines through. Tell yourself how far you have come and acknowledge the strength you never knew you had. Sit in a quiet place and talk to God. Express your full range of emotions. Your anger, frustration, and sadness, as well as your joy, relief, and optimism. Give thanks for the power to endure and carry on, for the new day and its promise, for all the blessings you have taken for granted.

Then brace yourself for the struggles that are yet to come.

CHAPTER TWENTY-TWO

The Never-ending Struggle

I LOVE action movies. Every time I admit this to people, they look absolutely shocked. How, they wonder, could a rabbi even be interested in such nonsense? But it's true just the same: I am mesmerized by movies like *The Terminator, Star Wars,* and, my absolute favorite, *Raiders of the Lost Ark.* To me these films are not just an escape from daily life; they highlight the heroic dimension of our existence. Our struggles are never-ending. The hero slays the alligator, only to face the snake pit. He or she manages to emerge from that pit only to confront the next obstacle, and the next one after that. Action movies remind me that the battle for life must constantly be waged.

One of the most common mistakes we make when we seek to overcome a tragedy is to assume that our struggle has an end. It doesn't. What *is* finite is the immediate period of deep suffering that follows a crushing blow. It might last a year, sometimes longer, sometimes less. But sooner or later the intensity of our suffering will subside.

However, the subsequent struggle for healing and restoration in our lives is endless.

Lisa, a woman in her early forties, came to see me one day. She began to cry as she asked me, "Why isn't my life getting any easier?" I asked her to tell me what was wrong. She said that her ex-husband Tim had been a philanderer and that living with his constant lies was utterly humiliating. Lisa had thought that leaving Tim would ease her pain. But she had been mistaken. Her divorce was an excruciating process. It meant that she had to leave the only man she had ever loved, and tear her family apart. It also meant that she had to put her daughter through absolute hell as she fought Tim in court for her custody. All through the long and ugly battle Lisa kept telling herself that once the divorce was over she would finally find relief and happiness. But just as her life was returning to normal, she was suddenly beginning to see that living on her own as a single mother without a date in sight was an entirely new form of agony. "I know that I'm better off without Tim," Lisa said, "but it doesn't mean that my life is getting any easier, does it?"

Sometimes we make it through the first stage of suffering, breathe a sigh of relief, and say to ourselves, "At last it's over. I can get on with my life now." Then we look in front of us and realize that we are not equipped to enter the life that lies before us.

It's so easy to lose hope, especially when we have worked so hard to reach a certain point, only to confront a huge roadblock.

ONE OF MY FAVORITE biblical narratives is the description of what happens to the Children of Israel after the Exodus from Egypt. I love the way the story provides hope without ever offering any easy answers.

The Israelites had spent four hundred years in slavery and at last they were free! But before they had time to experience even a moment of relief, they suddenly came upon the waters of the Red Sea. Without a boat or a bridge in sight, there was no way to get across. To make matters worse, they turned around to see Pharaoh and the Egyptians in full battle gear chasing after them.

The people cried out to Moses and Moses cried out to God.

God replied, "Why are you yelling at me? Tell the Israelites to keep walking." Keep walking? Where were they supposed to go? Straight into the water? No one moved. They were trapped. The waves were crashing down before them, and the Egyptians were rushing toward them from behind.

A legend describes how one man understood what he needed to do. His name was Nahshon ben Amminadab. While everyone else was praying for a miracle, Nahshon decided to step into the water. Nothing happened. He walked on until the water reached his knees. Nothing happened. He continued until the water reached his neck. Nothing happened. He kept on going until the water came up to his mouth. Still nothing happened. He pushed forward until the water reached his nostrils, until he was about to drown. Suddenly the sea before him parted and the Children of Israel crossed the sea as if on dry land.

The Children of Israel were overjoyed as they made their way to safety, but their struggles weren't over. When they got to the other side of the sea, their challenge was just beginning. Before them stretched a forbidding desert with its promise of brutal heat, no shade and no water.

When we feel trapped, we believe there is no way out of our predicament. But there is indeed a way through any obstacle we face. We have to find the courage to take the plunge, to take not only the first step along that path but also the second and the third. We have to be willing to press on even when it seems we haven't made any progress at all, even when the water has reached our nostrils and there seems to be no point in carrying on. Eventually the waters will part, and we will see the dry land, the road that lies before us. And we must walk along that road until the next challenge comes our way.

. . .

The Turning Point

IN ORDER to live our lives fully, we have to be willing to push on into the unknown future. That is the meaning of the words "Let me not die while I am still alive." There will always be new challenges to face, challenges that will test us and that will certainly set us back. But when we stop trying, when we give in to despair, we have stopped living.

About six months after our initial tearful discussion, Lisa met a man, fell in love, got married, and is now pregnant. Lisa is overjoyed, but she also acknowledges that trying to blend two families together has been a daily struggle.

A PRAYER

Why can't I ever find peace, God? I've been fighting for so long, and each time I think I'm done, a new battle arises. Will my struggles ever end? Renew my strength, God. Restore my hope. Give me the courage to stare down adversity and the faith to face whatever may come without fear and without despair.

Amen.

CHAPTER TWENTY-THREE

The Challenges of Daily Life

OUR MOST PERSISTENT CHALLENGES are often the least dramatic ones—not the life-threatening illness but the one that drags our spirits down; not the loss of our jobs but the daily pressures of our work; not the divorce but the constant struggle to sustain and revitalize a marriage; not the death of a loved one but the hostile relationship we can't seem to repair. How can we continue on a healing path when our lives are constantly in turmoil?

In February of 1996 I gave birth to our daughter Noa. When she was two weeks old, Rob and I bought our first home. We had exactly thirty days to pack up all our possessions and move. Adi, our two-year-old son, was going through a difficult phase. He was dumbfounded by our decision to keep the new baby. As far as he was concerned, I should have shoved her back in my belly where she belonged. When he wasn't sulking, he was hitting and biting. One morning he grabbed the telephone receiver, held it over Noa's skull, and politely asked me, "Mommy, can I hit it?"

Noa, for her part, was the poster child for colicky infants. She cried around the clock. She slept at sunrise; then, at nightfall, when I was about to collapse, she was ready to party. And what a party it was. Night after night without even a hint of sleep. Sleep deprivation combined with my raging hormones and I soon found myself crying at the strangest moments. I remember sitting in the movie theater with my son watching *Pocahontas* and streams of tears were running down my cheeks. When my husband asked me what was the matter, I replied with a quivering voice, "Pocahontas is so sad."

I was also having quite a difficult time nursing my daughter. I had recurrent bouts of mastitis, a painful breast infection, and was running a high fever, but a lactation expert told me to continue nursing; that it was the only way to clear the infection. I was told to use hot compresses before nursing and cold compresses after nursing. The lactation consultant recommended frozen peas. I was puzzled. I asked her what eating peas had to do with anything. She laughed and said the peas weren't for eating, they were for icing. There I was, lying on my back with a bag of Jolly Green Giant peas on each breast. And my daughter had to nurse every two hours! So just as the peas were coming off, the hot towels were on their way back on. Friends of mine said, "Nomi, you're crazy to keep nursing. It's obviously not working for you." But then I'd talk to lactation experts and they'd make me feel as if bottle-feeding were a form of child abuse. As if feeding my daughter Similac were like feeding her arsenic. So I continued. Another specialist suggested that I try to feed my breast milk to my daughter with an eyedropper. In a mad rush I ran out and rented a breast pump, then I raced to the drugstore and bought a bunch of eyedroppers. I got back to our apartment, and threw the eyedroppers in a pot of boiling water just as my husband was coming home from work. He walked through the door, took in the scene before him, looked at me as if I were insane, and asked, "Nomi, what are you doing? The only thing you feed with an eyedropper is a wounded bird. Noa isn't a wounded bird, she's a healthy baby." I looked back at him and suddenly started to laugh and cry so hard that I could barely breathe.

Finally, I decided to wean Noa. I made the decision with

more than a little ambivalence and guilt. I felt as if I hadn't tried hard enough. Perhaps I could have done more. Perhaps I had given up too fast. Perhaps I was lazy. Perhaps I was letting my daughter down.

But weaning was no simple matter for someone as prone to infection as I was. One counselor told me to bind my breasts with Ace bandages. Another told me to ice around the clock. A third promised me that cabbage leaves would do the trick. She explained that the leaves have the property of relieving breast engorgement. Eager to be done with this mess, I ran to the supermarket and bought a bunch of cabbage heads. Then I peeled a few large leaves off and placed them inside my bra. Miraculously, the cabbage did seem to take down the swelling. The only problem was that I had to go pay a visit to someone who was ill that day. I left the cabbage leaves on, and as I sat at the woman's bedside she kept sniffing around as if trying to identify a familiar scent. "Naomi, do you smell something funny in here?" she finally asked. "It's me," I confessed. "I smell like a bowl of coleslaw." I went on to tell her all about my nursing woes. I think my story really cheered her up.

In the midst of all this, the movers were coming the very next day. Rob and I tried to pack up all we could, simultaneously entertaining our two-year-old and our newborn. When the movers arrived, half our apartment was still not packed. We sent our furniture with the clothes still in the drawers. By the end we were literally scooping up armfuls of stuff and simply throwing it onto the moving truck. By nightfall, safely ensconced in our new home, we both breathed a sigh of relief and got the kids ready for bed. But suddenly we smelled something foul. "Adi must have a dirty diaper," I thought. But I checked and it was clean. "Perhaps it's Noa's." But she too was clean. Then I walked into the bathroom. Raw sewage was backing up into the sinks and the bathtub. Out came the yellow pages. We spent the rest of the evening with the Roto-Rooter man, who told us that we needed to replace our entire plumbing system.

In the morning, after another sleepless night with Noa, I decided to get acquainted with the new neighborhood. I was driving down a small side street when I heard the siren. A policeman on a motorcycle pulled me over and said, "Do you know what you did?" I said, "Yes, Officer, I think I didn't come to a complete stop at the stop sign." He looked at my beat-up 1980 Volvo, at my disheveled hair, at my pale skin, at the dark circles under my eyes, and said, "Get out of the car." I did. He put his finger in front of my face and said, "Follow my finger." I started to laugh. Not a good idea. Then I said, "I'm not drunk, Officer." He said, "You let me be the judge of that." I followed his finger. He said, "With your eyes, not your head." I started to laugh again. Nervous, I thought of trying to explain about the baby and the sleep deprivation, but he didn't look as if he was in the mood to listen. I thought about saying I was a rabbi, but then he would have been *certain* I was drunk. To his dismay, I passed the intoxication test. Finally, he wrote out a ticket and said I'd be getting a bill in the mail.

The very next week was Passover. Returning to the synagogue after two months of maternity leave, I was faced with the enormous task of getting myself and our community ready for the holiday. I had sermons to write, two kitchens to make kosher, and four Passover Seders to conduct—one for my family, one for my congregation, one for the children of the synagogue, and one for the senior citizens of Venice Beach. There were scores of questions of Jewish law for me to answer: "Can Pyrex be made kosher for Passover?" And "Is Coca-Cola kosher for Passover?" And "Rabbi, I know you can't eat bread on Passover, but can you eat cookies?" Not to mention the ten bags of mail I found waiting for me which had accumulated over the two months of my leave. Or the fifty boxes of books and clothing and toys I had to unpack and go through at home.

I was so busy at the synagogue and at home that I hardly noticed that I never did get that bill for the traffic violation. I shrugged it off, assuming that the Los Angeles bureaucracy was slow and that it would soon arrive. After another month had passed, I started to suspect that the bill might have gone to our old address, so I decided to call up to find out what to do. I got in touch with the traffic court, and when the woman on the other end of the line typed my name into her computer, she cried, "Oh dear, there's a warrant out for your arrest." "What?!" I screamed. She said, "You heard me. If an officer pulls you over for any reason at all, you're going straight to jail." "What am I supposed to do?" I asked. She said, "You have to come down to the courthouse and schedule a court date." "A court date?" I cried. "All I did was roll through a stop sign." She said, "You'd better do it right now."

I quickly got dressed and drove—extremely carefully—to the traffic court. I kept imagining a picture of my face on the wall of the post office and all of my congregants gasping at the sight of their outlaw rabbi. When I got to the courthouse, I asked the clerk, "Can't I just go to traffic school?" "Traffic school?" she repeated with a tone of absolute disdain. "You've got to appear in court before the judge." My court date was set for the next day. I decided that it would be a very good idea to take Noa with me. I fantasized that the judge would take one look at my beautiful infant, be filled with compassion, and immediately dismiss the charges against me.

After another sleepless night, I got out of bed, dressed my daughter in her cutest outfit, and headed off to court. There were dozens of people waiting, but the infant trick worked perfectly with the bailiff, who let me be the first person in line to see the judge. There was hope. I walked up to the bench and, to my dismay, the judge stared at me without even noticing the adorable baby in my arms. Before I had a chance to open my mouth, he said, "Ms. Levy, how do you plead?" I said, "Guilty,

Your Honor. I didn't come to a complete stop at the stop sign."
He said, "And why are you here today?" I said, "Because I was
waiting for a piece of paper that never came." He said, "You
shouldn't have waited. You should have called immediately. Is
there any overriding reason why you didn't?" Then he added,
"Like a hospitalization?" I thought of telling him about my colicky infant and my shell-shocked two-year-old. About the bags
of frozen peas and the eyedropper. About the new house and
the cabbage leaves, about the Roto-Rooter guy, the sleepless
nights, and about my life as the rabbi of a congregation. But
then I realized that though I felt besieged, I was merely overwhelmed by life's simple aggravations, not tragedies. And there
were fifty people seated behind me waiting to be heard so I said
nothing and paid the fine.

SOMETIMES life spins out of control and all our efforts to
move toward a higher plane of faith and tranquillity fail. That's
what happened to me during those first few months of my
daughter's life. The whole world seemed to be conspiring
against me. I started to feel like I was jinxed—the truth is that I
was just losing perspective. I was sleep-deprived, hormone-
filled, and overworked. But life's blessings were all around me
and I forgot to take the time to acknowledge them. I had two
healthy children, a loving husband, a new beautiful home, and
an intimate and caring congregation. I didn't end up in jail and I
am eternally grateful that the stop sign I ran didn't lead to a far
more tragic end.

Our daily lives will forever be full of challenges. There will
inevitably be setbacks that cause us to lose our footing. But we
must force ourselves to remember how far we have already
come and to acknowledge that we have the power to get
through this difficult time as well. It will pass. And we will find
ourselves climbing higher and higher.

A PRAYER

When I panic, God, teach me patience. When I fear, teach me faith. When I doubt myself, teach me confidence. When I despair, teach me hope. When I lose perspective, show me the way—back to love, back to life, back to You.

Amen.

CHAPTER TWENTY-FOUR

Transforming Ourselves

A TRAGEDY is not always a single painful occurrence. Sometimes our suffering is the result of a long accumulation of frustration and unhappiness. We may feel as if a disaster has struck when nothing in our lives has changed. There is no misfortune to point to, no event to hang our sorrow on, no way to articulate the source of our pain to our family and friends, or even to ourselves. Yet we still find ourselves feeling angry, sad, bitter, despondent. We may have all the symptoms of grief without being able to identify an obvious cause. Perhaps we are grieving for all the potential that we have failed to realize. Maybe all the compromises we have made over a lifetime have suddenly caught up with us. Perhaps we have come to a realization that our lives lack meaning; that we are leading a shallow, passionless existence. Or maybe we have just become painfully aware of how little time we have left and how much we still hope to accomplish. Is this not a catastrophe? Of course it is. An unlived life is a tragedy, too.

But we have within us the power to remake ourselves, to transform our lives, overcome our fears, realize our dreams, uncover our passions. We have the capacity to reclaim our hope and to fulfill our highest potential.

Most of us think of potential only when looking at children. We see a child and say this one's going to be a doctor or that one's going to be a musician. But we rarely speak about potential when we think of ourselves. We see ourselves as fully formed, and too often dismiss our hopes and dreams and yearnings as mere fantasies. Adults assume that the time for realizing all that we can be has passed. But no matter what our age, we *all* have the potential to change and grow.

I know this because I have witnessed it. I have seen congregants completely alter the course of their lives in the face of overwhelming odds. I can remember my own skepticism as they revealed their seemingly futile hopes to me, and I can also recall my utter amazement as I watched them turn those very fantasies into reality.

My congregants have taught me that we can dramatically change our lives no matter what our age. But in order to change, we have to be able to look honestly at our lives and experience our own dissatisfaction. We have to allow ourselves to fully feel our hunger for a better life. I have also learned from them that there is another prerequisite for transforming our lives: the ability to uncover a deeply held longing. If we're unhappy but have no direction or passion, we have nowhere to go. They have taught me that change involves risk-taking. We have to be willing to leave the security of our present lives behind in order to step into an uncertain future. And we also have to be willing to face failure. If we're not willing to allow for the possibility of failure, we're not going to be able to take a dramatic step into the unknown.

ED WAS in his early forties and had recently been divorced. He started coming to synagogue services about four years ago. At first he seemed a bit timid because he was new to Jewish life, but he quickly became one of the regulars. He joined various committees and was even voted Volunteer of the Year.

Ed had been a production manager in the entertainment

business. He put together the lighting at shows and concerts. For eleven years he traveled the world with rock bands on tour, working with everyone from Alice Cooper to Tony Orlando and Dawn. When I asked him if he ever got to listen to great artists, he told me that the wonderful musical experiences were few and far between. When he was on the road with a band, even a very talented band, he heard the same songs night after night in the same order, with the same cues. He said that it got very boring, which surprised me. I always thought that rock concerts were more spontaneous than that. But he explained that everything that happens is timed. Even the little comments and jokes the singers make between songs, the lines that cause the audience to explode and cheer, are all rehearsed and recited over and over and over again. For Ed, working with rock bands meant "having to listen to a lot of idiots telling you what a bad job you're doing."

Ed spent four months on tour with a famous hard-rock band. Every night of that tour the lead singer—who was always high—would call Ed into his dressing room to yell at him about some lighting problem. On the last night of the tour Ed walked into the singer's dressing room to thank him and tell him that he'd had a wonderful time traveling with the band. But the singer looked at Ed and said, "Who the hell are you? How did you get in here?" He had no idea who Ed was.

Ed traveled with Joan Baez, Blondie, Hall and Oates, Aerosmith, Nazareth. He worked in Las Vegas doing two shows a night with one singer for four months. The repetitiveness of it all was intolerable to him. After eleven years in the music business, he decided to leave that world behind. The constant travel and the abuse from spoiled stars had finally gotten to him.

Ed landed a position managing auto shows. The work was a lot less exciting, but it meant that he could live at home and actually have weekends off. Soon, however, he discovered that this new career was mentally easy but emotionally draining. It was draining because it was unfulfilling. He was making a lot of money, but he took no pleasure in the work he was doing. Nevertheless, he received outstanding job reviews and raises year after year. But eventually Ed's poor attitude began to surface at work. He would get into clashes with people and not care about how he was perceived. And one day, after eight years on the job, he was fired.

At that moment Ed had two simultaneous thoughts. The first was: "Oh my God, what am I going to do?" And the second was: "Thank God." Deep inside, Ed was relieved. But he still felt very low. He had lost all ambition. Friends of his would say, "Do what you love." But Ed would respond, "There's nothing that I love."

One day he was talking to a friend who asked him what he would really want to do if he had the opportunity. Ed replied that he had always wanted to be a lawyer. He loves nothing more than arguing—and he thought it would be great to make a career out of doing that. But as soon as he confessed his secret wish, Ed discounted it. "I can't do that," he said. "I'm forty-two years old." So he decided to start looking for another job in the lighting business.

Then the Jewish High Holy Days rolled around and Ed found himself at a service where I gave a sermon about my father. I talked about how he had longed to change his life but died before he ever got to realize his dreams. Ed told me that he sat in the synagogue and thought, "Is she talking to *me*?"

The next week Ed decided to give it a shot. He comforted himself by saying that he could always go back to lighting if it didn't work out. He took his LSATs. As he sat in the examination room, he froze. He couldn't understand the words before him. They didn't even sound like English. When he got his scores back, it was no surprise to him that he had done quite poorly. But somehow he gathered up the nerve to take the test again. He studied feverishly, and this time he did superbly. All the schools he applied to suddenly wanted him. Some even offered him a scholarship.

At the same time, an entertainment company offered him a position as vice president, with more money than he had ever made before. It was a wonderful opportunity, but Ed turned it down. Instead, he enrolled in law school.

School was difficult, but Ed loved it from the start. For the first time in a long time, he was actually using his mind, having exciting discussions with people, doing independent research. Every time a professor mentioned something—even as an aside—Ed would run to the library and spend hours exploring the issue.

As I write this, Ed has just completed his first year of law school. Although he's a little disappointed with his 81.5 percent average, he's proud of his achievement. He still has a long way to go, and some people think he's crazy to have given up a lucrative position for an uncertain future, but Ed has never been happier.

During summer break Ed has been working two jobs as a law intern. "I'm getting paid nothing, but I can't wait to get to work," he explained with a smile. "I used to get paid a lot of money, but I couldn't stand going to work."

THERE IS a price to pay when we set out to transform our lives. In Ed's case, he had to listen to and then ignore the many people who kept telling him what a dreadful mistake he was making. It's hard enough to overcome self-doubt when taking such a huge risk with our future. But when those who are closest to us start criticizing us, we have to gather up enormous courage not to be swayed by their assessments of us.

Sometimes the price we must pay when we set out to fulfill our longings is not just criticism; we may have to face shame and gossip or even the possibility of being ostracized from our own community. The cost of realizing our dreams may be high, but the rewards are immeasurable.

I USED to watch Leah week after week at Sabbath services. She came to pray, but I think she had other motives for being there. Leah had a thick head of long curly auburn hair that she seemed to be hiding behind, as if it were a curtain she could peer through. She always sat alone and always seemed to be scanning the room for an eligible bachelor. In her late thirties, she was quite successful. She had everything she wanted, except what she wanted most—a baby. Leah loved children and she was so good with them, but there was a problem—there was no man in her life. She dated, she went to singles events, she waited, she hoped, she prayed, but nothing happened. Eventually, she stopped coming to synagogue. I was sad to see her go, but I suspected that she left because she had not gotten what she had come for.

A number of years later, Leah phoned me. She was clearly elated and told me that she'd like me to preside at her daughter's naming. I was excited too. I asked her what the child's Hebrew name was going to be and what the father's Hebrew name was. With trepidation in her voice, she said, "There is no father." She told me that she had gotten pregnant through artificial insemination. Taken by surprise, at first I didn't know what to say. Then I told her that I would of course name her child. On the day of the naming I had mixed emotions. After all, a single woman having a child through artificial insemination isn't exactly a common occurrence. But as she walked into my study holding her precious daughter, all my hesitations melted away. She looked positively radiant. All the worry and the desperation had vanished from her face. I started to tear up as I held her child in my arms to bless her. This was a woman who had gathered up her strength and had chosen to remake her life despite the stigma attached to that decision. Somewhere deep down inside of me I believe that now she will soon find the man she has been looking for. She is so much more at peace, so much more ready to meet someone on her own terms.

THERE ARE PEOPLE who experience unhappiness and frustration not because of their own failure to realize their life's dream, but because others prohibited them from realizing it. One man in my synagogue was musically gifted as a child, but his mother never allowed him to pursue his gift. She pressured him to follow a more practical career path. There are scores of individuals whose deep longings have been thwarted by family, by a discriminatory society, even by religion.

We *do* have the power to recapture our longings and to realize them. It is never too late to do that. By breaking down the barriers that others have placed in our way, we are able not only to set out for a new future but to rectify a wrong that was committed against us in the past. It was Goldie Shore who taught me this lesson.

Five years ago Goldie approached me after services. "Rabbi," she said, "I'll be eighty-four this year and I want to have a bat mitzvah." I said, "Of course, Goldie. But it's not going to be easy. You're going to have to study with me every week for a year." She said, "This is something I've always wanted for myself. And besides, what do I have better to do?" The very next Tuesday, Goldie showed up in my study with a big shopping bag filled with papers, fruits and vegetables, a handkerchief, a sweater, a scarf, a Bible, two pairs of eyeglasses, another sweater in case it got chilly, and a tape recorder—not one of those small handheld models but a big old heavy one about the size of a large shoe box. I asked, "Goldie, how did you *get* here with such a heavy bag?" She answered, "With my feet. I walked." Then she sat down and told me all about her childhood in Europe.

How she wanted to learn Torah with her brothers but was not allowed. "It's not for girls," the rabbi told her. So she used to stand by the door and eavesdrop as her brothers studied. As a result, she picked up bits and pieces of Hebrew and prayers. One of her brothers became a Torah scholar, but when she tried to get him to teach her, he too refused, using the same refrain: "It's not for girls."

Week after week Goldie faithfully appeared at my door with her heavy shopping bag. The work was not simple. There was the Hebrew reading to master, as well as all the blessings and the melody of the haftorah. Not to mention the fact that Goldie had difficulty hearing. But she kept toiling away. One time it was cold and rainy outside, so I called her and said, "Maybe we should skip this week." But the next thing I knew there she was at my door. She said, "I've waited eighty-four years to hear Torah from *inside* the door, and I'm not going to miss a class now." Then Goldie added, "I want you to know that I take your tape with me to bed. It helps me to fall asleep when I have indigestion." I told Goldie how well she was progressing and she replied, "I know. I've got talent, don't I?"

Goldie had more than talent, she had a real gift. She was one of my best students. It was as if she had known the material before, as if she had learned it once and now all she needed was to simply refresh her memory.

When the bat mitzvah day arrived, three of her children and four grandchildren flew in for the occasion. Goldie was beaming. At the appointed time, she slowly made her way up to the pulpit. Wrapped in a tallis, a prayer shawl, she opened the well-worn text she had studied from for a year, looked out upon the congregation with the mischievous smile of someone who is about to share a secret, and began to chant. Her chanting sounded like music from another world. It was as if all the women of her generation who had never been permitted to chant our prayers were rolled up into one voice. A voice that seemed to say, "I am here."

A PRAYER

You have blessed me with many gifts, God, but I know it is my task to realize them. May I never underestimate my potential, may I never lose hope. May I find the strength to strive for better, the courage to be different, the energy to give all that I have to offer.

Amen.

Transforming Our Minds

ED, LEAH, AND GOLDIE are constant reminders to me that altering our circumstances can heal our pain. But change doesn't always lead to growth or to blessing. It can also be a curse that leads to emptiness and stagnation. One congregant of mine keeps dating and dumping girlfriends. Change isn't helping him, it's preventing him from ever taking the time to develop any meaningful relationship or achieve any level of real intimacy. All too often we worship change without ever noticing that it's not solving our problems. We keep buying new cars, new TVs, new wardrobes. We keep feeding our bodies without ever noticing that it's our souls that are hungry. We frequently assume that satisfaction is something we can acquire. But the deepest levels of satisfaction can only be achieved through sacrifice. We can change our jobs year after year without ever gaining an instant of satisfaction. One woman I know keeps changing her body parts in the hope that it will boost her self-esteem. She has a new nose, new breasts, new cheekbones, new teeth—and her same old low self-esteem.

Too often we fantasize that fulfillment will be found elsewhere—in fame, in wealth, in a new career. But we may be mistaken. The route that is most likely to help us transform our lives is the one that is the least explored. When the path toward healing cannot be found in any other arena, it is probably because it is located in the very place we are standing. Our life's mission may very well be hidden in the simple routines that we have come to devalue. Sometimes the only way to fulfill our highest potential is by staying put and transforming our thoughts. *Transforming* our lives doesn't have to mean *changing* our lives. It can mean returning to the same life but with new purpose.

Is our life's fulfillment staring us right in the face? Does it reside in our own homes? Is eternal meaning lying dormant in the marriage we have stopped caring about? Is it found in the curious eyes of the child we are always too busy to play with?

In the Talmud there is a legend that the Messiah is a beggar who sits on the ground binding his sores. Of course, people never notice him because they are looking for a majestic figure who will save them. The lesson we are supposed to learn from this story is obvious: our redemption resides among us, but we rarely perceive it.

SOON AFTER my father's murder, I began secretly hoping that my mother would remarry. She seemed so lonely and unhappy; I thought a new man in her life would cure her of her suffering. But my mother showed absolutely no interest in meeting men.

Unlike so many widows and widowers who eagerly attend all sorts of social gatherings in the hope of meeting a mate, my mother seemed thoroughly opposed to the idea of ever dating another man.

My desire for her to remarry grew much stronger as I was preparing to leave home for college. It's hard enough for any parent to face the prospect of an empty nest. But it had to be overwhelming for a woman who had once been a happily married mother of four to now face the idea of living all alone.

Before long my mother found herself alone in the home that had once been filled with constant commotion and laughter. The sadness of her solitude was intense. She would eat her meals standing up because she couldn't bear to sit down to an empty table. She would go to sleep with the radio on because she couldn't stand the silence. Even the thought of simply going to a museum by herself was intolerable.

I kept praying that Prince Charming would appear and wipe away all my mother's sorrow. My sister and I started talking about ways to introduce her to men, but nothing ever came of our plans. My mother seemed resigned to living out the rest of her days alone. There were many men who pursued her, but she ignored them. I thought her unwillingness to date was an unhealthy sign, and I even told her once that I thought she was deifying my father and refusing to live in the present. She told me that my father was the great love of her life and that she had no need to find any other. She added that most men of her generation expect a woman to take care of them, feed them, and clean up after them, and she wasn't eager to enter into that kind of arrangement. Even after our discussion I worried that my mother was trapped in a permanent state of grieving. But I was wrong. She would eventually find a way to transcend her sorrow. She did it not by finding a man to carry her away from her pain, but by actively choosing to endure the very solitude that had been causing her so much pain.

For a long time I saw that my mother's solitude was a source of great agony. But then it gave way to a sense of acceptance. Not of resignation or defeat, but a capacity to embrace the reality before her. My mother would never have chosen a life of solitude on her own. But now that it had come her way, she chose to live it to the best of her ability. She eventually gathered up the strength to part with my father's belongings, which had remained untouched in his closet since the day of his death. She began to gain confidence by managing her own finances, a skill wives of her generation never had to learn. Although a college graduate, at the age of sixty-five she began taking courses at Brooklyn College and quickly became a source of inspiration to many of the undergraduates who were her classmates. Every day she'd pack up her heavy textbooks in a canvas bag and take the city bus to the Brooklyn College campus. One course of hers was in conversational Yiddish. In the middle of the semester the professor became ill and was unable to continue teaching. My mother, who spoke Yiddish, was asked to take over the class for a session or two until they could find a replacement. She was so well received that she was asked to continue teaching for the rest of the semester and was honored at the faculty luncheon. She made new friends and reconnected with some dear childhood friends. Over the years she was blessed with ten grandchildren who have become a perpetual source of pride and delight. Three years ago, at the age of seventy-two, my mother decided to sell her home in Brooklyn where she had lived for over forty years and purchase a condominium in Brookline, Massachusetts. My mother's move from Brooklyn to Brookline was nothing short of a miracle. To be honest, I was the one who was having difficulty parting with my childhood home. My mother was excited to be rid of it, to be starting out on a new adventure. In no time she quickly acquired a whole new circle of good friends. She became an active member of a synagogue, where she began taking classes. She joined a walking group and began strolling out in nature. She takes courses at Boston University and volunteers each week at a rehabilitation center. She's so active that it's virtually impossible to get her on the phone.

I had thought that my mother's refusal to remarry was a sign of weakness and fear. But she showed me that it was actually evidence of her awesome strength, defiance, and courage. By embracing her solitude, she found a path to deep meaning and joy.

There is holiness and meaning hidden in even the most painful circumstances, even in the most mundane tasks. Instead of seeking to escape from our lives, the challenge of our existence is to find the capacity to uncover that holiness.

But to unearth the sanctity that is buried within our daily drudgery requires deep attention and discipline.

PART FIVE

Disciplines for the Rest of Our Days

What happens to our thirst for strength and meaning, for hope and healing, *after* a crisis has passed? People often turn to faith when a tragedy strikes, then forsake it when life returns to normal. But it is normal, everyday life that is our greatest challenge. The majority of our days on this earth are spent in unspectacular moments. Yes, we may have lived through trying times that have tested our strength and will. But the goal of our lives is not only to stand up to pressure and pain, it is to turn the mundane moments into spectacular experiences, to approach life not with fear or apathy but with awe and wonder, to perceive holiness in the most common encounters, and to find God in the least likely places. What follows are practices to take with us into the rest of our days.

CHAPTER TWENTY-FIVE

Opening Our Eyes

GREAT AND UNEXPECTED MIRACLES are sometimes standing right in front of us, but we can't see them.

Hagar and her son Ishmael were wandering alone in the desert when they ran out of water. Hagar was tired and frightened, lost and alone. Ishmael was dying. Hagar laid her only child down beside a bush because she could not bear to watch him die before her eyes. After she set his body down, she burst into tears. Suddenly an angel of God called out to her and told her not to fear. The angel promised Hagar that Ishmael would not die; that he would grow up to become the leader of a great nation. Then a wondrous thing happened. God opened up Hagar's eyes and she saw a well. The bleak picture before her melted away in a single moment of insight. She ran to the well and brought Ishmael water, and he was revived.

The miracle that God performed for Hagar and Ishmael in this story is very subtle. God didn't *place* a well in Hagar's path. The only miracle God performed was to open Hagar's eyes so she could see what had been standing right before her all along. The well had been there from the start, but she was too delirious and panicked to see it.

Why can't we see the blessings that surround us? Because much of the time we are either too busy or too preoccupied to stop and look. Sometimes we are in so much pain that when we *do* look we don't see clearly. Or we are so used to feeling cursed that we can't believe that the blessing before us could possibly be intended *for* us. We can be so focused on a specific goal that we fail to notice that the solution to our problem cannot be found on the path we have been so feverishly pursuing. Rather, the answer lies in the place we have ignored. Our blessings are often right before us. All we have to do is stop and take notice.

I WAS TWENTY-SIX YEARS OLD when I became the rabbi of Temple Mishkon Tephilo. After an article appeared in the *Los Angeles Times* about a young, single woman rabbi in Venice, I couldn't help but notice that a whole lot of single men were suddenly finding God. I definitely wanted to meet a man, fall in love, and start a family, but I was also wary. My first marriage had taught me that love is not always enough to make things right.

Being a rabbi, I knew it would be even harder to meet a man. Most people tend to put their religious leaders on a pedestal, believing that they are the embodiment of piety, goodness, and wisdom. I wanted to find someone who didn't think of me as a rabbi, who was able to accept me with all my flaws, and who was not afraid to show me his. For this reason I thought it would be a bad idea to date congregants. But eventually, I made an exception to my rule.

He wasn't exactly a dues-paying congregant. We met accidentally in the hallway of my synagogue, where he had come to meet a friend. But overnight he discovered the merits of religion. He came to every service, every class, and offered to walk me home from synagogue. I was so determined not to have any feelings for him that I invented all sorts of reasons for his frequent attendance. I wondered if there was something the matter with him, what spiritual pain he might be in. I thought to myself, "I wouldn't go to synagogue as often as this guy does, and I'm a rabbi!"

Then I began teaching a midday class entitled "Love and Torah." On the first day of class, several mothers from the preschool showed up. As I began to teach, one more person walked in. It was him. In the class we tried to distill the Bible's vision of love, examining the love of Adam and Eve, of Abraham and Sarah, of Isaac and Rebecca, of Jacob, Rachel, and Leah. We talked about passion and the lust of Samson and Delilah. We studied the beautiful intimacy that David and Jonathan shared. And we spoke about the love of God and of God's love for humanity. Then we began to read aloud from the Song of Songs, the sensual biblical love poem attributed to King Solomon himself, a dialogue between a man and a woman.

The man in the poem says to his beloved:

You have captured my heart, my own, my bride, you have captured my heart with one glance of your eyes, . . . Sweetness drops from your lips, O bride; honey and milk are under your tongue; . . . A garden locked is my own, my bride, a fountain locked, a sealed-up spring. Your limbs are an orchard of pomegranates and of all luscious fruits, . . . fragrant reed and cinnamon, . . .

The woman responds:

Awake, O north wind, come, O south wind! Blow upon my garden, that its perfume may spread. Let my beloved come to his garden and enjoy its luscious fruits!

The following week we read these words spoken by the man:

How fair you are, how beautiful! . . . Your stately form is like the palm, your breasts are like clusters. I say: Let me climb the palm, let me take hold of its branches; let your breasts be like clusters of grapes, your breath like the fragrance of apples, and your mouth like choicest wine. Let it flow to my beloved as new wine gliding over the lips of sleepers.

The woman responds:

I am my beloved's, and his desire is for me. Come, my beloved, let us go into the open; . . . Let us go early to the vineyards; let us see if the vine has flowered, if its blossoms have opened, if the pomegranates are in bloom. There I will give my love to you . . . I would let you drink of the spiced wine, of my pomegranate juice. His left hand was under my head, his right hand caressed me. I adjure you, O maidens of Jerusalem: do not wake or rouse love until it please!

Week after week, the moms and the man returned. Soon he started bringing delectable treats to class. One week it was fresh ripe strawberries. Then he began bringing the sensuous fragrances mentioned in the Song of Songs. The first week he brought frankincense, the week after it was myrrh. I didn't know such things even existed in the modern world. The words of the poem were working like a love potion. I began to open my eyes, to see him not as a religious fanatic, or someone in need of my help, but as someone lovingly trying to get my attention.

What happened to me? How did I suddenly let the man who would soon be my husband, the man I had been ignoring for months, into my life? My favorite verse from the Song of Songs is this: "I am asleep but my heart is awake, the voice of my beloved knocks." That is exactly what I was going through. Even though I was out of touch with my emotions, my heart was totally awake, and it heard and felt all of Rob's subtle—and not so subtle—advances.

Then one day a miracle happened. I opened my eyes. Suddenly I felt all the feelings I had been suppressing for months. As I looked upon the man before me, I saw in him a soul mate, a lover, a life's partner. He asked me if I wanted to go have some coffee with him.

Eyes wide open, I said yes.

A PRAYER

Open my eyes, God. Help me to perceive what I have ignored, to uncover what I have forsaken, to find what I have been searching for. Remind me that I don't have to journey far to discover something new, for miracles surround me, blessings and holiness abound. And You are near.

Amen.

CHAPTER TWENTY-SIX

How Can We Learn to Open Our Eyes?

THERE ARE TIMES in life when, like Hagar, we are granted a moment of rare insight. That's what happened to me when I finally saw Rob. Unfortunately, we can't rely upon such miracles. Life is too short to spend it waiting for God to pry our eyes open. We have to learn to open our own eyes to the many blessings that God has given us. There are many steps we can take that may heighten our awareness of miracles, of blessings, of God's holy presence, when we usually see nothing more than life's daily drudgery.

I think the most powerful are night vision, rest, and breath.

Night Vision

WHEN WE'RE IN PAIN, the last place we want to be is alone at night. "How am I ever going to make it through the night?" we ask ourselves as darkness descends. During the day we lean upon a myriad of distractions to lessen the sting of our pain. But as the world around us begins to grow still, the world within us starts to stir. This inner world is filled with turmoil, with thoughts we'd rather push away than deal with, and feelings we'd prefer to ignore rather than acknowledge. It's as if we have two separate personalities. By day we are confident and rational; by night we are vulnerable and shaky. By day we are atheists. By night we believe in God and goblins and ghosts and spirits.

But as much as we may dread darkness, it is also a great teacher.

Night teaches us humility. It reminds us that we are not invulnerable, that we are small and frail and mortal, part of nature's great and unchanging rhythm. As much as we'd like to defy its pull, we must, like every living creature, eventually give in to the darkness. No matter how many lights we may have on, or how long we may try to stay up and watch TV, we must all inevitably concede and let go.

Night teaches us that we are more complicated than we think; that we have the power to dream great dreams, as well as the capacity to wish for terrible things.

Night teaches us how to pray. During the day we rarely have the need or the time to talk to God; at night we find ourselves whispering secrets to God as if to a close and trusted friend. I don't think it is an accident that most of the Bible's prophets encountered God only at night, for night teaches us to be more receptive to the world of the spirit, to miracles.

Debbie was sitting beside me at synagogue one Saturday when suddenly she confided in me that, fifteen years earlier, she had once heard God speaking to her. She had started to date John and they'd hit it off right away. Debbie fell head over heels for him. The first time they made love, she heard a voice in the darkness saying, "This man will be the father of your children." She heard the voice so clearly that she opened her eyes and looked around to see who was speaking. But no one was there. Instantly she felt that God had said it. Debbie married John and they have since brought four beautiful children into this world.

Scores of perfectly sane people have told me about encounters they have had with deceased loved ones in the night. Were they all just dreaming? I don't know. Night offers us a bridge to spiritual realms that are unreachable by day.

Night forces us to rest, to reflect, to regroup. To be still. To stop running and hiding.

Most of all, night teaches every one of us—the sinner, the cynic, the sufferer, the tortured soul—that we are capable of rebirth. It calls to mind the darkness of the womb from which we all emerged and urges us to remember that we too can re-create ourselves out of that same darkness. It reminds us that we have the power to enter the darkness, face our deepest fears, and emerge whole and new and reborn.

There is one problem with all of this, though. We might be reborn in the night, but when morning comes we wake up and pretend that nothing really happened to us. We wipe the sleep out of the corners of our eyes, the fears out of the recesses of our minds, and the prayers out of the depths of our souls. Only when we are willing to embrace the side of us that dwells in the night can we begin to experience the world with an openness and a capacity to perceive and receive the many blessings that God bestows upon us every day of our lives.

Molly is a dear friend of mine. She's not one of my congregants because she's not Jewish, she's Episcopalian. But she dubs herself an honorary congregant because she spends so many of the Jewish holidays at my family's table. She is an extremely witty, sharp, talented, and successful writer. When she was sixteen, her parents left town for a weekend. Molly and her siblings were so excited to be home without parental supervision that they invited all their friends over for a wild party. The next day, as they were cleaning up the mess from the night before, a neighbor came over to tell Molly that her father had been rushed to the hospital. She jumped into her neighbor's car and together they sped off to find her younger brother, who was out riding his bike. When her brother looked back and saw the neighbor chasing him, he started pedaling his bike faster and faster, trying to escape. He was sure he was being pursued because he was in trouble for throwing the party. Molly watched her brother trying to race away and thought to herself, "It's too bad he can't run away from this."

In the hospital Molly's father was dying from a cerebral hemorrhage. Although he had dark brown skin, he looked pale and his lips were blue; Molly started rubbing his arm, trying to warm him up, but there was no way to get the chill out of him. Hours later he died.

At his funeral, a very traditional, two-day Southern ceremony with an open casket and a viewing room, Molly thought to herself, "What are we doing here? He's not *in* that body." She couldn't understand why her family was staring at an empty shell. "This is exactly where he's *not*," she thought. "This is the one place where I *know* he's not." She would rather have been anywhere but there at the funeral home. She longed to escape to the lake, where she could still almost see her father tinkering with the sailboat he loved, where she could still hear his laughter and smell his cigar.

During the months following her father's death, Molly felt utterly alone. She had to reorient herself day after day and remind herself, "Oh my God, this is really real." She had adored her father beyond description. He was wise, loving, funny, and firm. He was everything to her. She missed him so much.

One night she fell asleep. She hadn't been sleeping long when she felt a hand on her shoulder, near her neck. The hand gently shook her. She was lying on her stomach and she turned her head to see who was standing over her. No one was there, but she had a very strong feeling that it was her father. Her heart was racing. She felt him saying, "I'm here. You're going to be all right."

It doesn't matter to Molly if this encounter with her father was real or if it was only real to her. "Whether I dreamt it or whether it was an actual event, the effect on my life was the same. He was with me and I was going to be OK."

Molly went through a very dark period during the years after her father's death. She felt lost, angry, extremely frightened. But that mysterious encounter created a sense of well-being inside of her. Amid all the turmoil in her life, there was now her father's assurance to anchor her. She was grounded by that experience. It taught her to believe that her father would be with her always.

WHEN YOU ARE about to lie down tonight, turn off the lights and the television and the radio. Don't be frightened. There is nothing in the dark that you can't face head-on. The darkness may magnify your pain, but know that there is an *end* to pain. Trust that it will give way to joy. To awe. Allow your mind to wander. Don't fight the tears if they happen to come. Feel the prayer on your lips. Pause for just one moment to take in the night—and let the power of the night take you in, too.

A PRAYER

As the holy darkness descends upon me, I offer this prayer to You, my God. May the peace and the holiness which I feel this night remain with me always. May my fears give way to faith and may my pain soon give way to laughter. And may the lessons of the darkness fill my days with awe so that I may learn to experience You, my God, all the days and nights of my life.

Amen.

The Power of Rest

IMAGINE what it might feel like to take a day out of each week and spend it in pure restfulness—not a day to get our errands done or go out to the movies or the mall, but a day when we restore our souls. The Bible tells us that God created the world in six days and that on the seventh day God rested and was revived. The Bible views rest as a divine activity, not as a sign of laziness or weakness but as a sign of holiness and wisdom.

Recently, while driving down the street, I saw a huge billboard advertising a kick-boxing class. It said: "You Can Rest When You're Dead." What an insidious concept. It speaks volumes about our society. We are in such a hurry to succeed, to pack each moment with adventure, that we don't leave ourselves any time to enjoy, to reflect, to rejoice, to be grateful. To rest.

How much have we missed because we hurried? Because we never took the time to notice? Whom have we neglected? When we rest, we don't *miss out* on life, we learn to *appreciate* life. But how many of us ever take the time to enter into *real* rest? Not just vacations or time to spend on hobbies, but a regular discipline that can change our very selves.

Judaism has its own unique perspective on the Sabbath, our day of rest. Beginning every Friday at sunset, we celebrate it until it ends Saturday night. People tend to think of the Sabbath as a day of prohibitions: you *can't* do this and you *can't* do that. But it's really a day of *privileges*. It's a day when we leave our week behind and enter into a new plane of being.

A Sabbath day is a way to take one day out of each week and live it differently. In peace. It is not only a time to stop work, it is a time to stop *thinking* about work (making mental calculations is work, too). It is not a restriction, it is a freedom. Imagine what it might feel like to stop spending money, to stop looking to the outside world as a source of entertainment and distraction. A day of rest gives us the opportunity to find true relaxation from within. For too many of us, our usual guests are our nightly TV personalities. Aren't there other people we could be welcoming into our lives? How about our own families? How about friends we have lost touch with? How about God's holy presence?

Making time for rest replenishes our souls no matter what our faith. How would our lives change if for one day each week we were to leave the world of materialism and technology behind and enter into the world of spirituality, nature, and beauty? Picture a day when we allow ourselves to rejoice in physical pleasures. A day of good company, wonderful food, fine wine, perhaps even romance. What might it feel like to treat ourselves royally once a week, to set the table with the best china, to put beautiful flowers in our homes, to light candles, to take the time to pray to God? Picture a day that we spend not by fretting about the past or by worrying about the future, but by living in the sacred present. A day in which we can be still, still enough to actually hear the things we so often miss: the silent yearning of our souls which we usually deny or ignore. A day to be still enough to hear what it is that the people in our lives are *really* trying to say to us. Still enough to appreciate all the gifts and blessings that we take for granted each day, still enough to feel God's presence in our lives. Imagine what it might feel like to let go of all the cares of the week, to allow our bodies and souls to relax, to welcome in the peace and the joy and the holiness and the light of true rest.

SOMETIMES I look at a couple and think to myself: "They've got it all." That's certainly what I thought whenever I saw Amy and Matt. I had watched their love blossom; I had performed their wedding ceremony. They seemed to have everything one could desire: love, looks, money, success.

One day they came to see me, worried about their relationship. They were constantly bickering and their sex life was virtually nonexistent. They worked extremely long hours at high-pressure jobs and looked seriously stressed. They were tightly wound, very different from the way I had seen them when they were falling in love.

I asked them how often they had the opportunity to really enjoy time together. Their response was: hardly ever. At night they were so exhausted that when they were alone, they just fell asleep. During weekends there were so many errands to catch up on that they were constantly on the go.

I asked them to try to experience a Sabbath day to see how it felt. They looked at me as if I were insane. Amy and Matt were not observant Jews, they came to synagogue once a year. I said, "You asked for my help and this is my advice." I suggested that one day a week, starting on Friday at sunset, they should try doing something radically different. They should leave the workweek behind and allow their spirits to be revived. They looked extremely apprehensive. I explained that they didn't have to do it for the rest of their lives—only for one Friday night.

The next week Amy and Matt came back to see me. I watched them as they strolled into my office, arm in arm. They told me they had taken my advice and that they hadn't experienced such peace since their honeymoon. They seemed like different people, calm, patient, and affectionate with each other, grateful for the gift of time they had suddenly gained.

TRUE REST doesn't affect us only when we are resting. It spills over into our weeks, our years, our very lives. The days preceding the day of rest become days of excitement and expectation. Even the most harried workdays become tolerable when you know a day of holy peace is shortly arriving. The days succeeding the day of rest become days of light, too. They shimmer with the afterglow of a revived spirit.

True rest gives us a completely different perspective on all of life's difficulties. It allows us to heal, to reflect, to give thanks, and to face whatever lies ahead with a renewed sense of calm.

A PRAYER

I long to change the world, but I rarely appreciate things as they are. I know how to give, but I don't always know how to receive. I know how to keep busy, but I don't know how to be still. I talk, but I don't often listen. I look, but I don't often see. I yearn to succeed, but I often forget what is truly important. Teach me, God, to slow down. May my resting revive me. May it lead me to wisdom, to holiness, and to peace.

Amen.

Breath

THE HEBREW WORDS for "soul" and "breath" come from the exact same root.

At the beginning of creation, the Bible tells us, God's spirit hovered over the water. When God created the human being, God breathed into its nostrils the breath of life and it became a living being. Every breath we take is a reminder that we are divine creations infused with an eternal spirit. All too often we take this simple truth for granted.

How we breathe defines how we live. If we hyperventilate, we live in panic. If we take shallow breaths, we lack energy. If we take deep breaths, we live in calmness and ease.

Moses appeared before the Hebrew slaves after his encounter with God at the burning bush. He told them that God had sent him to free them from their enslavement. But because of the hard labor they were forced to endure and because of what the Bible calls "short breath," the slaves didn't listen to Moses.

Their reaction is understandable. When we are overworked, we lack the ability to see salvation, even when it is staring us in the face. We lose perspective and have no time to think. We're too overwhelmed to notice the life around us.

The "short breath" that prevented the Israelites from hearing Moses is also a metaphor for impatience of spirit. When we are impatient, we breathe quick breaths that limit our awareness and prevent us from tuning in to our surroundings. Jewish tradition teaches us that angels possess an ease of breath, a calmness, as they approach God's holy presence. Unfortunately, none of us is an angel, but we *can* learn to take deeper breaths that may help us to better experience the holiness that resides right inside our very beings and all around us.

In a meditation class I taught a few years ago, I asked my students to close their eyes and take slow, deep breaths. There was a man in the class who simply couldn't do it. He kept looking at his watch and tapping his feet. The minute he would close his eyes and try to breathe slowly, he would fall asleep.

This did not surprise me. So many of us have only two switches: we are either active or asleep. We don't know what it means to be awake and at rest. We don't know what to do with ourselves in a moment of stillness. Fidgety and anxious, we want to talk, act, move about, break the intensity. But if we can allow ourselves to welcome the stillness, if we can allow ourselves to breathe deeply and fully, we will gain insights that can never be acquired through motion.

A single breath separates the living from the dead. One single breath. I can vividly recall that sacred moment when each of my children was born. That deafening silence as I waited for the baby that had just emerged from my womb to take its first precious breath.

Silence . . . and then that wonderful wailing and gasping.

I can just as vividly recall the sound of my father's respirator as it forced air into his lungs. And the moments when I have sat by the bedsides of the dying. A shallow breath, another shallow breath, and then nothing. Silence.

A single breath is the barrier between life and death. We who breathe without ever thinking need to remember that the breath we take is the spirit of God that animates us. If we can learn to appreciate our breath, we will begin to appreciate our life and the God who gave us that life.

A Breathing Meditation

EVERY FRIDAY NIGHT I do a breathing meditation. It helps me to feel God's presence within my being and to appreciate the gift of life that I often take for granted. Here is how the meditation works:

Take a slow, deep breath in. Feel a warmth entering your being. Now breathe out slowly. Imagine that you are releasing all the cares of the week. All the tension. All the worries. All the sadness. Spend the next few minutes taking long, full breaths.

Each time you inhale, imagine that you are filling up your every limb with lightness, like a helium balloon, so that with each breath you are gradually floating higher and higher. Each time you exhale, imagine that you are releasing the heavy weight that burdens your soul. Remember to breathe deeply and slowly.

Breathe in peace, breathe out anxiety.
Breathe in light, breathe out darkness.
Breathe in joy, breathe out pain.
Breathe in health, breathe out sickness.
Breathe in trust, breathe out fear.
Breathe in rest, breathe out panic.
Breathe in the life breath that comes from God, breathe out all that we take for granted.

Take a moment now to thank God for something you forgot to thank God for today.

CHAPTER TWENTY-SEVEN

Finding a Mentor

THERE IS one more way for us to learn how to open our eyes. We can find a mentor.

There is an ancient rabbinic teaching that every person should find a master. I think it's sage advice. We all need to learn from someone who is wiser than we are. Someone who has more experience, objectivity, and insight than we have.

It is time to find our mentor when we are ready to see this world with new eyes, when we are ready to let someone else show us a perspective on life that we might never have arrived at on our own. Acquiring a mentor requires a certain level of humility—a capacity to look up to another person and to place yourself in the role of disciple. And it also requires a certain level of confidence—a capacity to retain your own unique identity in the face of the mentor's instruction.

A mentor doesn't have to be an old man or woman with graying hair. It can be someone much younger than we are. I remember when a woman in her thirties, widowed a few years earlier, began to offer advice to a man in his seventies who had just lost his wife. I marveled at how this older man looked to this young woman for answers, for guidance, for comfort.

The presence of a mentor in our lives has the power to improve our existence immeasurably. But how do we find the *right* mentor? The one who will not lead us astray.

There are plenty of people who claim to have the answers to our problems. But the right mentor is someone who will lead us to insight and teach us wisdom, not someone who will predict our futures or tell us exactly what to do. A mentor seeks not to own us but to gently support us. In the Bible it is easy to recognize the characters who are destined for greatness: it is usually the man or the woman who least wants the job, the one who feels the least worthy, who turns down the position and tells God to look elsewhere for a leader.

Once I was sitting in on a class that a colleague of mine was teaching. A student raised his hand and asked what seemed to be a very basic question. The rabbi, my colleague, responded, "I can't answer that question now. Only after you have studied with me for five years can I begin to share that information with you." The rabbi's response annoyed me. It said more about his need for power than it did about the question being asked. What he was really saying to that student was, "I hold the keys to secret information that you cannot acquire without me. You must become my disciple, you must make me your master, in order to uncover the answers to your questions."

But then you meet someone like Sam and you know you're in the presence of a humble master, a master of biblical proportions.

I met Sam at the very first service I ever led at Mishkon Tephilo. To say I was nervous would be an understatement. All these people had come to check out the new curiosity. Who was this woman rabbi? What kind of rabbi would she be? Was she some kind of radical? Did she hate men? I was so jittery my knees began to shake. I managed to clench everything from my jaw to my fists in order to stop shaking, but my knees had a mind of their own. I took a deep breath, stepped into the lobby of the sanctuary—and encountered Sam. He was just my height, with white hair that encircled the rim of his bald head. He looked at me with surprise and said in a Yiddish accent,

"You're the rabbi? You look like a little girl." My confidence took yet another nosedive.

Sam is the synagogue's shammas, its sexton. For over thirty years, tending to the shul, he has seen rabbis come and go. He has remained the one constant in a synagogue that has seen its congregants turn over dozens of times. Sam stayed on even when the synagogue could barely get a minyan, a prayer quorum, on the Sabbath. And he stayed on even when the synagogue took one of its riskiest steps—hiring a woman rabbi.

After that first encounter in the lobby, I worried that Sam might not approve of me. Some of the older members of the congregation were up in arms because of my hiring. A few left the congregation over the decision, and those who stayed were not exactly all staunch supporters. One congregant accused me of preaching polytheism; another was concerned about my menstrual cycle, viewing it as a time of impurity. She took me aside and whispered, "Rabbi, how can you stand on the pulpit with your period?" Still another went around telling people, "Guess what? My rabbi wears a bra!"

When the service was through, the skeptics encircled Sam, waiting for him to pass judgment. "She really knows her stuff," he said. And then he continued, "When I was growing up in Europe, my grandfather was too busy to teach me, so I studied with my grandmother. She was a very learned woman." Sam's seal of approval was as good as gold. I was accepted into the congregation with open arms.

Strictly speaking, Sam was my employee. The job of the shammas is to make life easier for the rabbi. But I could never bring myself to ask Sam to do anything. How could I, a twenty-six-year-old nobody, order this man around? He knew far better than I did about what needed to get done.

Sam shared the pulpit with me at every service. I would lead the early part of the service, then he would read from the Torah. The juxtaposition of the two of us always felt so perfect to me. I was a woman in my late twenties, he was a man in his late sixties. My presence on the pulpit pointed to the fact that our tradition was changing. Sam sang with the accent and the melodies of a rich past. His deep, resonating voice conjured up images of the shtetl and of a world that is no more.

Usually when people try to imagine what a mentor or a guide might be like, they envision a person who exudes a calm and serene spirit, like Buddha, or a cross-legged guru sitting atop a mountain, or Yoda in *Star Wars*. Sam is the antithesis of all that. He's always in a hurry. But behind the whirlwind there lies a presence that is steady and unflappable. His gaze is piercing, his memory photographic, his wisdom intense. His spirit is deeply religious, coupled with just as deep a sense of humor.

During the Holocaust, Sam endured humiliation, terror, starvation, torture, and brutality. Most of his family was slaughtered. But Sam rarely makes mention of his past, except with dark humor. After the powerful earthquake that shook Los Angeles a few years ago, sending highways and homes crashing to the ground, our entire congregation was in a state of panic, including its rabbi. But Sam just went on with his day as if nothing had happened. He said to me, "When you've lived through the Holocaust, there's not much that can scare you."

Before a Holocaust commemoration service, Sam once asked, "Rabbi, do you need me to be here?" When I told him no, he said, "I don't think I need to be reminded about the Holocaust. I think I can remember it well enough on my own."

What I've learned from Sam, I've learned not from any formal instruction. He has never sat me down and said, "I'd like to teach you something." I have been under his tutelage without him ever knowing. Watching him pray with such fervor—when his life experience has surely given him reason to believe in the *futility* of prayer—has taught me how to pray. When I watch Sam pray, I sometimes feel as if he's reminiscing with a dear friend. God and Sam have been through so much together.

Witnessing him chant from the Torah has taught me what devotion is all about. To Sam, a sacred text is a living force, it is the greatest mentor of them all—one worth living for when all hope is lost.

And listening to Sam's stories has changed my life.

I've heard Sam tell stories about his childhood, and visitations of spirits, and about great teachers. From his stories I've learned that there are holy lessons to be gained even from the least promising experiences. He has taught me the importance of asking for help when I'm in trouble instead of trying to solve all my problems by myself. From him I've learned the power of "simple" faith, of retaining the innocent faith of a child even in the face of great tragedy. Sam has taught me what humility is, and to never assume that I am invulnerable. He has taught me the lifesaving potential of humor. He has shown me that it is possible to laugh and find momentary relief even in hell.

Here are just a few of Sam's stories. I hope you will learn from them as I have.

The Labover's Lesson

SAM'S GRANDMOTHER spent all week preparing for the appearance of the great Labover Rebbe. She baked all sorts of special cakes and delicacies, and set the table with her finest white tablecloth and the special china she reserved for holidays. The Labover arrived, took a seat at the table, tasted a morsel of food, and said, "Madam, your cooking has the taste of the Garden of Eden." Just then a pauper appeared. That was no surprise. Beggars would often come looking for food. But this man was rude and loud; he reeked and was shabbily dressed. Sam's grandmother was unnerved by the disturbance. She led the beggar to the kitchen and gave him some food to eat. But he started to shout, "I don't want to sit in the kitchen. I want to sit at that nice table." He pointed to the Labover and cried, "I don't want to eat this stuff, I want what he's eating!" Without blinking an eye, the Labover stood up, took the man by the hand, led him to the table, sat him down by his side, and gave him all the food that was before him. The beggar gobbled it up like an animal. He didn't even use a fork, just grabbed the food with his hands and shoved fistfuls into his mouth without even tasting what was going in. Next, he proceeded to pour himself some tea but ended up spilling it all over the white tablecloth and breaking the teacup. Then he just stood up and, without so much as a "Thank you," ran out of the house, screaming and cursing all the while.

Sam's grandmother was beside herself. She had spent all week preparing for the rabbi's visit and now this rude lunatic had ruined everything. She started to cry. The Labover called Sam over and asked, "What do you think of this situation? Did you learn anything?" Sam replied, "Is it that the man forgot to say the blessing before he ate?" The rebbe said, "This may look like a spoiled occasion, but it's not. Every situation in life comes to teach you a lesson. There are three things that you should learn from what just happened. The first is this: It's no great accomplishment to welcome a pleasant person into your home—a kind, polite poor person, who is grateful and obedient. But to take in someone you don't like, someone who is rude and dirty, someone who stinks and shouts, that's a much higher form of kindness. The second thing you should learn is this: You shouldn't put poor people in some other room to eat by themselves. It might be more comfortable for you, but it's humiliating for them. Put the hungry at your own table and treat them like honored guests. The third thing to remember is this: Don't give away to the poor something you don't like. Don't just throw them some leftovers. Give away what you love. Give them what you would want for yourself. That's the highest charity."

"Every situation has a meaning," the rebbe continued.

"Nothing in life has no explanation. If you can remember these three things I taught you, then today wasn't such a bad day after all."

A Failed Job Interview

SAM'S GRANDMOTHER, who owned a small hotel, needed to hire someone with a horse and cart to run errands for her business. When a man came to apply for the job, she asked him this question: "What would you do if you were riding somewhere and a heavy obstacle was blocking the road?"

The man replied, "I would get out of the cart and move it out of my way." Sam's grandmother asked, "But what if it was too heavy to move?" The man responded, "Then I would try to steer the horse around it." Sam's grandmother said, "What if there was no way around it?" The man said, "Then I would have to turn back." Sam's grandmother said "Thank you," then showed the man out. When she closed the door, she told Sam that the man didn't get the job. Sam was puzzled. The man had seemed nice enough and he really needed the work. But his grandmother said, "He didn't give the right answer." Sam asked, "What did he say that was wrong?" His grandmother explained, "We don't live by ourselves in this world. If you're in trouble, you go for help."

No One Is Invincible

WHEN SAM was shipped to a ghetto called Tarnow by the Nazis, he learned that a relative of his, Moniek, was the local representative of the Jews in the ghetto. Moniek was responsible for the division of labor. The conditions in the ghetto were bleak. People were starving. They were shot down in the streets. Daily they were rounded up and shipped to Auschwitz. Sam went to see Moniek. Entering his apartment was like entering another world. There was expensive furniture. The guests were dressed lavishly. They laughed and chatted. Food was plentiful. There was even live entertainment, a woman singer. It was totally disorienting. Moniek hung his arm over Sam's shoulder and said, "You've got nothing to worry about anymore, kid. You're going to survive. I'll watch over you. I'm a powerful man." But a few days later there was a mishap—and Sam was sent off to a labor camp. As he was being led away, Moniek's sister cried over Sam as if he were already dead. She said, "Now there's no one left of my family." As he was telling this story Sam looked at me and said, "Can you imagine what it's like to have to listen to people mourning your death?"

Months later at the camp, Sam saw the woman who had been singing at Moniek's that first night. She told Sam that the entire ghetto had been liquidated and sent to Auschwitz. Moniek never made it, however. He had been shot in front of everyone on the street.

Humor in the Wake of Hell

AFTER LIBERATION, Sam made his way to a displaced persons camp for very religious Jews. A rabbi in the camp complained that there was no mikvah, no ritual bath. He told the UN relief workers that if they really wanted to help the Jews after all they had suffered, they would build a mikvah. Eventually he triumphed. The authorities installed a mikvah.

One day great news spread through the camp. A young couple was to be married! The UN relief workers organized the festivities. They arranged for strictly kosher food to be brought in and erected a wedding canopy. Traditional Jewish klezmer musicians were hired. On the day before the wedding, the rabbi's wife accompanied the bride-to-be to the newly built mikvah for her traditional prenuptial immersion. The two women went in, but after only a few short minutes they came out. "The wedding is off!" the rabbi's wife announced. When the bride had undressed for the ritual bath, the rabbi's wife saw that she was pregnant. As a result, the rabbi refused to perform the wedding. There was no way to appease him. He would not budge. There would be no wedding.

The following day there was an abundance of festive food in the camp, the musicians played on, but no wedding took place. The bride-not-to-be grumbled, "If only they hadn't built that damned mikvah!"

SAM HAS ALLOWED ME to peer inside a Jewish world that no longer exists, a world that has been obliterated. He has shown me that it is possible to return even from hell. He has given me countless lessons for living: how to get along with people, how to make changes without making waves, how to put the past *in* the past so that it doesn't invade the present. He's a model of untainted humility, of unwavering faith. He's been a father figure to me when I needed a father to turn to, yet he's also been an attentive congregant who taught me to believe in my ability to teach, in my capacity to be a rabbi. Most of all, he has taught me how to find humor in even the darkest occasions. How to use humor as a tool for healing.

Sam explained that sometimes if you separate a memory from its surroundings, instead of making you cry, it will make you laugh. It will give you the strength to carry on.

If I were to tell Sam that he's taught me any of these things, he'd think I was out of my mind. He's taught me effortlessly, without ever trying to impose or to educate. Without ever noticing that I've been watching and learning.

Just last week I was sitting in Sam's living room asking him all sorts of questions about his past. It was another warm sunny day in Los Angeles. All of a sudden I thought I heard rocks falling against the window. I got scared. I thought that somebody might be vandalizing his home. Sam didn't flinch. We walked out to his front porch and it was hailing! In Los Angeles! We both stood there in silent amazement. How could it be sunny one moment and hailing the next? That's a question that Sam stopped asking long ago.

A PRAYER

Grant me the humility, God, to seek out a master. The courage to ask for help. The discernment to distinguish wisdom from folly. The willingness to embrace new thoughts. May my learning lead me to insight, to reverence, to love, and to You.

Amen.

CHAPTER TWENTY-EIGHT

The Power
of Lifelong Prayer

PRAYER CAN BE an enormous source of comfort to us in times of tragedy and despair. But prayer also has the power to save us when all is going *well*. In fact, those times when we least have the urge to pray are precisely the times when we need to pray the most.

Prayer is a way to reach out to God, to share our deepest yearnings, secret wishes, even our unspeakable sins. Prayer not only connects us to God, it also forces us to become intimately acquainted with our own souls. Most of all, prayer helps us to remember our hopes—for ourselves, for our loved ones, for this world—and gives us the strength and courage to realize the dreams we most desperately long to achieve.

Prayer should never be viewed as a substitute for action. It is a *prelude* to action.

It's *hard* to talk to God. It's difficult to find the words or the voice to speak the words that are locked up within us. We have so much to say, but it takes enormous energy to dig deep enough inside our souls to reach out to God. So we *don't* pray and then we wonder why God seems so far away.

True prayer can only happen if we are willing to search for God with all our hearts and souls. When we're ready to listen with all our strength.

In the Bible the prophet Amos warns that a day will come

when there will be a famine in the land. This famine is not a hunger for food or a thirst for water but a longing for communication with God. I think it is fair to say that this frightening prophecy has been realized. We live in a time of spiritual famine. We have lost the ability to pray.

We are not the only ones who feel cut off. God, too, feels alone. In a moving passage in the Book of Isaiah, God cries out, "Why, when I came, was no one there, why, when I called, would none respond?" As the great philosopher Dr. Abraham J. Heschel taught, God longs for us. Not just when we're in trouble but every single day. God yearns to speak with us. God needs us. God daily asks: *Just take one small step toward me and I will meet you there wherever you are. No matter how far you have strayed.*

Prayer Requires Discipline

IT MAY BE TRUE that we can turn to God whenever we need God, but prayer requires discipline. The more we pray, the more profound and honest our prayer becomes. If we're in a relationship with someone but only start communicating when a crisis arises, we're in a troubled relationship. Relationships need constant nurturing. We have to talk all the time so that when times get rough both partners will know what to do.

The same goes for a relationship with God. Faith needs constant nurturing. And we can't get good at it without practicing. You can't just pick up a clarinet one day and start playing jazz, you have to practice your scales day after day. There's no way to get around it. You may be the most gifted musician in the world, but without practice you will never reach the greatness you're capable of. So too we may have faith in God, but if we never pray, we will never know the heights our souls can reach.

We don't have to be experts to know how to pray and we needn't speak volumes. Our prayers needn't be elaborate or formal, but they do have to be a deliberate reaching outward toward God and a deliberate reaching inward toward our deepest honesty. Prayer can be music, the melody we sing even if we don't have the words. It can be motion, movements that express what no words can ever communicate. A prayer can be just one sentence. One of the most beautiful prayers in the entire Bible is Moses' sensitive plea to God on behalf of his sister who has fallen ill. Moses begs God to heal her, but he doesn't use fancy language or praises to flatter God. All he says is, "Please, God, please heal her."

Prayer Requires Passion

THE GREATEST PITFALL of discipline is that it usually diminishes passion. It's easy to get passionate about something that is new and rare, but it's hard to get worked up about something we do day in, day out. Routine inevitably extinguishes romance. But prayer requires not only discipline, it requires passion, too.

I know plenty of people who pray daily with their mouths. They recite words and utter praises. That takes no great talent. Prayer, in this respect, is like making love. Some people can go through the motions with their bodies but their hearts remain closed and untouched. But to pray with intensity and fervor, with all your heart, with all your soul, with all your might—that's a huge feat. It's painful. It means that we have to open ourselves up.

In order to pray, we've got to be brutally honest. We must concentrate and meditate and shut out all distraction. Prayer isn't something we just *do*. It involves more than opening up a book and reading words; it requires that we delve inward until our very souls begin to whisper. As that whisper gains strength within us, we reach across the distance toward God.

We can put on a front with anyone in our lives. We can pretend that all is well, that we are OK. But there's no way to deceive God. Before God, we are all naked. Our secrets are exposed. And that's frightening.

It's natural to want to cover up, to hide. That's what Adam and Eve did in the Garden of Eden. God called out to them, "Where are you?" and they were hiding. But God calls out the same words to each and every one of us: "Where are you?" And we have to decide how to respond. We can hide or we can turn to God in all our nakedness, in all our frailty.

We have to remember that to stand before a God who knows all our secrets is not *just* frightening. It is also deeply comforting. It means that no matter how false our lives may feel, we are known and understood and loved.

There is a beautiful Hasidic story about a poor shepherd boy who came to pray at the synagogue of the great Hasidic master the Baal Shem Tov. As he sat mesmerized by the words and the melodies of the service, he had a deep longing to join in. But the boy was illiterate and didn't know any of the traditional prayers.

In his pocket the boy kept a small flute that he would take with him when he was tending his flock. Whenever he played the flute, any sheep who had gone astray would return.

The little shepherd sat in silence during the long and awesome service, but at last his soul could no longer restrain itself. He reached into his pocket and blew on the flute with all his heart. A commotion swept through the synagogue. The people who had been praying so intently were startled and appalled by the sudden outburst. But the Baal Shem Tov explained that the shepherd's prayer had come from the depths of his soul and had risen to the very seat of God. With his small flute, the shepherd had lifted up all the eloquent prayers in the sanctuary.

I have always loved this story because it reminds me that prayers must come from the heart; that words are just the vehicle for communication with God.

The moment we stop being self-conscious is the moment

when we can begin to soar. It's true in sports, in art, and in acting; it's true in love; and it's true in prayer, too. We can't connect with someone else if our minds are focused inward. We can't give or receive. We can't experience the power of true union in prayer, we can't meet God, without stretching outside ourselves. But it's very hard to leave our critical minds behind. We live in a culture that rewards us for staying in control. We're not supposed to seem too vulnerable or get too excited. But the most moving experiences we can have in prayer are the moments when we completely lose ourselves. When we let go of our wants. When we forget our personal petitions and enter into a dialogue with God.

Prayer Needs No Words

WHEN I WAS A CHILD, my family belonged to an Orthodox synagogue in Brooklyn. Each year when Yom Kippur arrived, my grandmother, mother, and sister would say goodbye to the men of our family and head up the staircase to the women's section. In Orthodox synagogues men and women do not sit together.

As a young girl, I was still allowed into the men's section. I would sit on my father's lap and stare inside the mysterious ark as it opened and closed. There was a white velvet curtain decorated with gold embroidery and jewels. To the side of the curtain hung a long golden rope with a tassel at its end. A man would be called, and he would walk up a set of steps, shake the rabbi's hand, and pull on the golden rope. The curtain would be gently swept to one side, revealing two beautiful hand-carved wooden doors. The man would then open the doors onto what looked like an enormous jewelry box. There were several Torah scrolls inside, each elaborately covered in white velvet, decorated in gold with jewels that caught the light, and with an ornate silver crown with tiny bells hanging down which tinkled when they moved. A large silver breastplate hung around the neck of each scroll. I desperately wanted to go up to the ark and touch one of these treasures, or at least to behold them close-up. But I soon learned that girls were not permitted near the Holy Ark, nor were they allowed to touch the beautiful Torahs. I also learned that soon, as I grew older, I would be banished to the balcony to watch the service from the women's section. It was then that I began to pray for the opportunity to be near those holy scrolls.

When I'd had enough of the men's section, I'd run up three flights of stairs to the balcony, where I'd usually find my grandmother weeping. That's how she would pray. I don't think she could read either Hebrew or English, but that didn't seem to bother her. She would cry all day. And in her tears there was an eloquence that no words could ever possibly capture.

Our rabbi's name was Rabbi Stein. He was from Poland and spoke English with a thick accent. He had a full head of white hair and a tired expression that seemed to be burdened with the pain of his entire congregation. To me Rabbi Stein looked ancient, but he was probably only in his sixties.

Rabbi Stein always spoke in a whisper that seemed to be pleading with us, "Listen." I can't tell you what Rabbi Stein was pleading about, because his sermons were always in Yiddish and I don't understand Yiddish. Listening to him deliver a sermon was quite an experience. He would get up before the community and whisper. Soon the whisper would grow louder, then he would start to get all worked up. Suddenly he'd start shouting and then he would weep. He would cry and sway and then he would fall silent.

I never understood a word he said, but I was sure that he was talking directly to God. I thought that Yiddish was God's mother tongue and that Rabbi Stein was telling God in heaven that we on earth are very sad and frightened. That we are hurt. When Rabbi Stein would start to cry, he always seemed so lonely, so small and vulnerable before the giant crowd of Jews who had come to hear his words. The sound of his voice spoke to me and touched me. You don't need to know the words to hear the voice of prayer, to be moved.

The only other occasion at which I heard Rabbi Stein speak was at my father's funeral. Some other rabbi got up and started to spout a series of platitudes about God's plan and how God wanted my father more than we did. I started to get very angry, but then Rabbi Stein appeared on the pulpit. He seemed much older and even more frail than before. He stood before my family and delivered my father's eulogy in Yiddish. I couldn't understand one word at my own father's funeral. You might think that this would have made me feel angry or alienated or left out. But it didn't really matter. To be honest, I was glad I couldn't make out what he was saying. I wasn't looking for words of comfort. No words could possibly have eased my pain. But the sound of his sad whisper spoke to me. As he uttered the words of the eulogy, I wrote my own eulogy in my heart.

Our synagogue took great pride in Rabbi Stein's scholarship. People would always say, "He has a fine mind, he's quite accomplished. He's from the old country but he has a degree from Columbia University." I am sure Rabbi Stein *is* quite a scholar, but what I will always remember about him is not his Talmudic argumentation but the passion of his prayer. All those years listening to him taught me that there is also a power in *not* understanding. His sermons in a language I could not comprehend taught me how to imagine and how to seek out my soul. How to talk to God. He showed me that the highest form of prayer is one that comes from the depths of one's heart.

Taking the First Step

WE DON'T HAVE to be learned to know how to pray. We don't even have to be religious. All we have to be is willing to reach beyond ourselves.

We all know that prayer comes easily when we are in trouble and that it's harder to work up a desire to pray when all is well. But the hardest thing of all is to gather up the strength to pray after a tragedy has occurred. Anyone who has endured a tragedy knows this feeling. "Why bother?" you ask yourself. "What's the point of praying anyway? Does it do any good? Is God even *listening?*" I wish I had answers to these questions, but I don't. I don't know God's ways any better than you do. And so far, God has never dropped by to explain them to me. All I can do is to describe what prayer has done for me.

When my father died, I was filled with rage. I was angry with him for dying and angry with the doctors for not saving his life. I was angry with my mother for showing weakness, with the police for not finding my father's killer, and with my friends for pitying me. I was angry with adults for saying stupid things and with myself for feeling so helpless. I was angry with God for doing nothing. I was angry with the entire world except for the one person who rightfully deserved my fury: the man who pulled out his gun and shot my father point-blank for no reason at all. My father was as threatening as a feather. He was armed only with clothes and skin. He was five foot three and walked with a limp. He was so opposed to violence that he never allowed any of his four children to own even a water pistol. He was so gentle that he never raised a hand to any of us, ever, and so humane that he hated even verbal cruelty. To him the phrase "Shut up," a phrase so common that my four-year-old son has picked it up from Bugs Bunny cartoons, was the profanity of all profanities. My father deserved to receive nothing but kindness from others; instead, an evil person came and brutally took away his life. So why was I never angry with my father's murderer? Because it would have been like venting my fury at the air. The murderer was a nameless, shapeless, faceless figure. I couldn't direct my venom toward nothingness. It would have been futile.

God is shapeless and faceless, too, but to me God has always seemed as real as I am. That's why, after my father's death, I hated God. At the time, I believed in the God I had heard stories about in religious school: I pictured God as a powerful old man who sat on a throne in heaven and swooped down to protect the weak and innocent. And that God had let me down. At least that's what I thought. So I tried to stop believing in God. But that never worked. It was like trying to stop breathing—I could only hold my breath for so long.

But I *did* stop believing in the mighty and powerful Wizard of Oz version of God. Instead, I started experiencing a God who was neither a man nor a woman, a God who lived not in heaven but everywhere. And over time my hate gave way to other emotions: to sadness, to longing, to determination, to frustration, to acceptance, to hope, to awe, to love. Over time I learned how to start praying again. Not the prayers of my youth, when I expected God to save my world, when I thought I had the power to control my fate. But the prayer of someone who takes God as a given but God's actions as a mystery. I haven't stopped making requests. But I *have* stopped expecting automatic and predictable responses to my petitions.

Now I pray for strength and wisdom. I pray to God to heal the sick, to eradicate war, poverty, and disaster. I know full well that my prayers may not be answered in any direct way. I am asking for things that are humanity's responsibility, not God's. But I hope that God will give human beings the compassion, the courage, and the insight to repair and heal our world.

I also turn to God to simply offer praise and thanks. I pray each morning in gratitude for my life and for the new day. I also pray before and after I eat because it reminds me how fortunate I am to be blessed with food on my table. I prayed to God every day of my pregnancies. I cried out to God during labor (I cursed a lot, too), and I thanked God the moment both of my children were born. I pray to God every single night to watch over my two sleeping children and every time I get inside an airplane (I hate flying). I pray because prayer strengthens me; it reminds me to take nothing for granted, and it challenges me to strive for better. I pray because I have the *need* to pray. I have the desire to tell God my deepest fears and hopes, to articulate my innermost feelings and thoughts. I pray because I long to share secrets that I may never share with anyone else. Because I believe that God hears and understands.

My favorite words of prayer come from a famous Jewish prayer called "Adon Olam"—"Master of the Universe." "Adon Olam" is often the concluding prayer at Sabbath and holiday services. Most people look forward to it because it means that the long service is finally over. During "Adon Olam" people are frequently so busy thinking about getting out the door of the sanctuary that they pay little attention to the words of this great poem. These are its concluding lines:

> *Into God's hand I entrust my soul,*
> *When I sleep and when I wake.*
> *And with my soul, my body, too;*
> *God is with me, I will not fear.*

Whenever I feel confused or lost, this prayer always shows me the way back to God, to faith, and to peace. It reminds me that everything that I am, body and soul, is in the hand of God, whose presence fills the universe and who is as close to me as my own breath. And that no matter what this unpredictable world sends our way, with God by our side there is nothing to fear.

A PRAYER

Dear God, as I pray, day after unpredictable day, may the words of my lips spring forth from my soul. May I turn to You, God, in tears, in laughter, and in song. And may my prayers be answered.
Amen.

CHAPTER TWENTY-NINE

The Power of Ritual

IT WAS DUSK on a Sunday night. A group of us who had known Cody well were invited to gather at Joni's house. The truth is, I never liked Cody very much. He was a spoiled bully. But I felt bad for Joni. She had rescued him from the pound when he was just a puppy, and she had loved him the way a mother loves a child. She took him with her wherever she went, trained him, and showered him with toys. Cody was a hyperactive mutt with black and white spots. He often got into brawls with the other dogs in the park. Our dog Sophie, a small beagle, used to play with Cody, and we were always wary of her getting into a tangle with him. We had just seen Cody two weeks before and he had seemed as healthy as ever. But he had succumbed to a cancer that had traveled through him at a frightening pace.

At the appointed hour, we took Sophie with us and headed over to Joni's house. There was quite a crowd already in attendance. The people mingled and the dogs sniffed one another. Soon Joni called us all out to the front yard, where we formed a circle around the empty doggy bed. A few people spoke about Cody's endearing qualities, and Joni began to sniffle and wipe at her tears. Suddenly she turned to me and asked me to say something as a rabbi. I was stunned. I had never officiated at a dog funeral before and certainly hadn't studied pet burial in rabbinical school. But I didn't want to hurt her by refusing to speak, so

I quickly collected myself and spoke about the special relation-ships we are capable of having with animals. How they are loyal and giving and never critical. I told everyone that loss is always difficult, but it is also inevitable. Although the loss of a pet is not the same as the loss of a human being, it nevertheless hurts. And we should allow ourselves the time to mourn our losses. I told Joni that she had been a great guardian and friend to Cody, that she had given him a good life. He had received more love and attention than many children get in this world. And that she should treasure the time she had been granted with her dog.

By now it was dark outside. Joni handed out candles. She lit hers, then we went around the circle passing the light from one person to the next. We were ready for our procession. Joni led the way; we followed with our dogs in tow, in silence, by candle-light. We made a pilgrimage to the park where our dogs had played together. Joni guided us to Cody's favorite tree, where he used to leave his mark; then she pulled out a Maxwell House coffee tin that housed Cody's ashes. She sprinkled some of his ashes around the tree, and those who wished to took turns doing the same.

I'm not a dog person. I barely tolerate our own dog, and chiefly for my husband's sake. So as I took in this scene, I found it somewhat difficult to understand. "Only in Los Angeles," I thought. I have seen human beings buried with less commotion and emotion. I have also seen people buried without a soul to mourn them, and this snarling mutt was being eulogized as a saint. But by the end of Cody's ceremony, I started to see things differently. This dog funeral really helped Joni. It provided her with comfort, with a sense of closure, with an opportunity to bid farewell to a creature who had been her loyal companion. The ritual created a community out of all of us dog owners. We were no longer just people who hung out in a park together: we were bound together by our shared experience.

.   .   .

WE LIVE in a strange age. Many of us long for rituals that we have no access to. The religious rituals that our grandparents lived by have been all but forgotten. Many of our parents discarded them like an unwelcome inheritance.

In the Jewish community, abandoning the rituals of the past was not just a reaction against the primitive superstitions of religion: it reflected a desire to erase the outward signs of distinctiveness. In America, Jews along with many other immigrant groups wanted to be accepted as Americans, not as strangers who practiced a different faith. By abandoning ritual, Jews believed they could enter the predominant culture more easily.

But now, we who have been raised ritually naked yearn desperately to be wrapped in a mantle of meaning. We long for the structure, the holiness, and the shelter that rituals can provide. We have witnessed the emptiness of a solely intellectual focus. It has brought us little comfort and has deprived us of our sense of awe. It has furthered our knowledge but not our wisdom; it has fed our minds but not our souls. And so we find ourselves reaching out in an attempt to recover a birthright that has been discarded. Some of us, like Joni, are creating new rituals. Others are exploring the timeless rituals that lie within established faith traditions.

We are hungry for rituals because they give our lives a sense of drama and grandeur. They transform mundane routines into sacred encounters and give us a way to express ourselves without speaking. A ritual is a prayer that is articulated not with our words but with our entire bodies. It harnesses abstractions and transforms them into things that we can see and touch, taste and smell. It turns thought into action, faith into deed, devotion into practice. It's one thing to love a man with all your heart and soul, but when you put your lips to his, your emotions become a tangible reality, your body becomes the agent of your devotion, your love is manifest in a physical act that shoots straight through you into him.

It's one thing to remember God when we are dutifully sitting in a house of prayer. But it's another to remember God wherever we are. There is a wonderful story in the Talmud about a yeshiva student who was overcome by lust. The student was dressed in his traditional clothes including his ritual fringes, which observant Jews wear to remind them of God's commandments. He went to see a prostitute and when he walked through the door he found six beds covered with silver sheets and a seventh covered with golden ones. There were silver ladders leading to the first six beds, and the seventh ladder was made of gold. Next, the prostitute sat down nude on the seventh bed. The yeshiva student also undressed, but just as he was preparing to have sex with the prostitute, his ritual fringes flew up and smacked him across the face, and he came to his senses.

I wish the holy objects in our own lives could give us a good slap every now and then. Their presence is supposed to accomplish the same end. They are here to remind us of our highest ideals.

Performing a ritual is like kissing God. At last we are able to experience our love not only with our souls but with our bodies, too. That deeper level of connectedness cannot be established in the mind: it has to be realized in the flesh.

On the day of my rabbinic ordination, I heard my name being called. With a mixture of excitement and trepidation, I stepped up to the podium. The chancellor of the seminary was on my right, and the dean of the rabbinical school was on my left. Together they spread a prayer shawl, a tallis, over me. As I stood there wrapped in this simple square of cloth, I felt connected to God in a way I had never known before. I felt sheltered, protected, enveloped in God's holy love. No diploma could have created the magic that tallis produced. No words could have induced the holiness that tallis engendered.

When we take part in a religious ritual, it connects us not only to God but to those who share our commitment, to those performing the same ritual across the globe. And it also binds us to those who performed this exact same ritual centuries ago, and to those who will perform it centuries after we've gone.

Rituals of mourning are the most carefully observed rituals of all. People want to receive the comfort that these rituals provide; they have a need to reach out to God when they are feeling empty and alone. They long for structure and predictability when their lives have been shattered and thirst for meaning when all meaning has been lost. They yearn for the company of a community that will lighten their burden.

But as in the case of prayer, we rarely seek out rituals when we most need to remember God—not during a crisis but every single day.

Getting Started

WHEN PEOPLE come to me for advice about where to begin their explorations of ritual, I always tell them to start with daily prayer. I suggest they say a prayer of just one sentence in the morning the moment they rise and another in bed when they are about to fall asleep. These prayers form wonderful bookends for our days. They help us to approach the new day with an awareness of God and our potential to bring goodness into this world, and they also help us to approach the night with a sense of awe rather than fear.

Thanking God for our food is another daily ritual that can infuse great meaning into our lives. Eating is no great accomplishment. Every living thing needs food to survive. But when we eat after we have uttered a blessing to God, we can no longer just shovel food into our mouths without thinking. Our eating becomes a sacred deed, an acknowledgment of the gift of food which God has given us. A preservation of the holy bodies God has given us.

People often ask me for suggestions of rituals that can help them keep the memory of the dead alive. Remembering our departed is similar to the challenge of remembering God. In both cases, we are seeking to preserve what we cannot see or touch.

Lighting a candle on the anniversary of a loved one's death is one way to preserve his or her memory year after year. It is a Jewish custom to light a memorial candle at home on the anniversary of a family member's death. The candle burns for twenty-four hours and is a reminder of the life that is no more and of the light that continues to shine upon us which even death cannot extinguish.

Another ritual that can be enormously helpful, especially to those in need of healing, is immersion in water. Water has the power to revive us in a way nothing else can.

Water not only revives us; it transforms us. In the Bible, the Jewish people were born the moment they passed through the parted Red Sea. Before that, they were just a band of freed slaves; after they emerged from the water, they became the People of Israel. If we enter a body of water in the right frame of mind, we can exit with a new sense of purpose and self.

Most faiths use rituals involving water as a way to purify and revive the soul. The mikvah, the ritual bath, is where Jews go to achieve that experience of rebirth. A mikvah is any natural body of water or a structure that contains natural flowing water. Personally, I prefer the ocean to the indoor mikvahs. It's riskier because it can get quite cold and because you have to be totally naked—no clothing, no jewelry, no nail polish, not even contact lenses may be worn. There can be no barriers between you and the water in this ritual. Just the same, I have spent many shivering, life-altering moments in the Pacific Ocean.

Beth came to me looking for a way to spiritually cleanse herself of the past and mark the beginning of a new era in her life. I suggested a mikvah in the ocean.

I met Beth at the beach at the break of day. Not a soul was out. The mist hung heavy over the water, the seagulls squawked above us. We walked slowly into the waves. It was cold, but it was the kind of cold that leaves you feeling refreshed, not numb. When the water was waist-high, I held up a sheet and Beth got undressed. When she was ready, Beth plunged into the water until it covered her completely. When she surfaced, she recited the blessing over immersion. She submerged herself again, then recited the blessing over new beginnings. Beth was sopping wet, her hair was sticking out in all different directions, she had no makeup on, her eyes were red from the stinging salt water, but she looked indescribably radiant, purged, pure, whole, reborn.

PART SIX

Coming Full Circle

As time passes, we will find ourselves further and further removed from the immediacy of our pain. We will continue to look back at it—but from an ever-changing perspective. Healing is not exactly like climbing a ladder: it's more like climbing an unending spiral staircase. As we ascend, we return to the identical point in the circle where we had been before, but we are now standing on a higher landing. From above we see the same experience but with new eyes. Details blur, and a deeper meaning may unfold before us.

In time we may come to rethink the assumptions we had once made about our lives and our pain. We might come to see that death is not as final as it once seemed to us. That healing is never as complete as we might have liked it to be. That God is not as useless as God appeared to be at the time of our suffering. And finally, that we are far, far stronger than we had ever imagined.

CHAPTER THIRTY

Beyond Memory

MOST PEOPLE envision heaven as a euphoric place up in the sky somewhere. Beyond the clouds. Over the rainbow. They believe that the souls of the dead ascend there after death.

But what if heaven isn't that far from us? Isn't God everywhere? Why should an eternal soul that comes from God be banished to some distant stratosphere? Maybe memory *isn't* the closest thing we have to those we have lost. Perhaps the souls of the dead are closer than we think. Perhaps they are among us.

My mentor, Sam, told me that his father had been a very sad and angry teenager who couldn't make peace with his mother's untimely death. One day he ran away and enlisted in the Austro-Hungarian army, something unheard of for a Jewish young man of that era. In the army, it was impossible for Jews to keep kosher or to observe the Sabbath.

It was Yom Kippur, and Sam's father was very depressed. He had just ended his shift on the night watch when he saw a figure off in the distance. It was his mother. He was sure of it. He chased after her, but she kept running away. He kept calling, "Mama, why did you die so early? Why did you leave me?" But his mother didn't answer. She kept running away, and he kept chasing after her. Running and crying. When he couldn't run any farther, he fell to the ground, exhausted and panting. He laid his face, wet with tears, in the dirt and drifted off to sleep.

When he woke up, he found himself miles away from his army camp. There was a pillow of freshly picked wildflowers beneath his head. He stood up and saw a fire glowing in the distance. He met a man passing by and asked him for directions back to his army unit. The man responded, "Didn't you hear? That camp was bombed last night. Nobody survived." From that day on, Sam's father stopped resenting his mother for abandoning him. He believed that she had come back to save his life.

A Sanctuary Full of Souls

I REMEMBER the first time I walked into the sanctuary of Mishkon Tephilo. I couldn't figure out how to turn the lights on, so only one tiny light shone in the entire cavernous space—the eternal lamp that remains perpetually lit over every Holy Ark in every synagogue across the globe. As I stood there taking in the scene, I felt that I was not alone. I sensed that I was in the presence of souls who, over the decades, had prayed in that sanctuary. The room seemed to be saturated with souls, with the murmurings of the ages.

Over the next few years, whenever I stood before the congregation each Sabbath, I always felt that I was standing not only before God but before all the souls who had once belonged to the congregation. The synagogue's deceased rabbis seemed to be with me as well. I wondered what they thought of me, of my teachings. I wondered if they approved of sermons given in a soprano voice. Somehow sensing their presence gave me the strength to carry on even when I felt frightened, burned out, or just bored.

Is it far-fetched to feel surrounded by souls we cannot see? I don't think so. Judaism is full of such tales. Elijah's spirit is welcomed on Passover and at every circumcision ceremony. On each of the seven nights of the festival of Sukkot, a different patriarch is summoned to come and pay a visit: Abraham, Isaac,

Jacob, Joseph, Moses, Aaron, and David. In the Bible, King Saul went to a witch to conjure up the spirit of the Prophet Samuel. Hasidic literature is full of accounts of visitations. The Talmud and the Midrash both speak about visitations of souls as well. Once a rabbi named Rava was sitting by the deathbed of Rabbi Nachman. Rava asked Rabbi Nachman to visit him after his death. And sure enough, not long after Nachman's death, he appeared before Rava. Rava asked Nachman if death was painful. Rabbi Nachman said that it was as painless as removing a strand of hair out of a cup of milk. But he added that if God were to ask him to return to the world of the living, he would not consent, because the fear of death is so overwhelming.

My favorite place to pray was always in that same darkened sanctuary of Mishkon Tephilo. Sitting all alone in the dark, I would pray to God and imagine all the prayers that had been whispered in that sacred space: prayers of thanksgiving, prayers for healing, prayers of the broken-hearted. The tear-filled prayers of the bereaved and the song-filled prayers of rejoicing.

I had a congregant whose daughter had died some twenty years earlier. Every year, as the High Holy Days approached, this woman would buy two tickets to the service: one for herself and one for her deceased daughter. As I'd look out at the community every Rosh Hashanah, I'd see her sitting there with that single empty seat beside her. And I believed with all my heart that mother and daughter were united in prayer and in love.

I. B. Singer once said that when someone close to you dies, they feel far from you. As far away as anyone close can ever be. Only with the years do they become nearer. And then you can almost live with them.

I love Singer's way of thinking about loss because it perfectly describes the relationship I have with my father. When he first died, I felt completely alone and abandoned. But over time he has taken up residence in my life. By now you can almost say that he's a squatter. He won't leave me alone. I don't mean that I actually see or hear him, I just *feel* him with me. It is an unmistakable feeling of being in his presence. It began when I was in college, and at first it frightened me. I didn't *want* to be flooded with thoughts of him. But gradually, I welcomed him into my life. Joyous occasions used to be times of great pain in my family. Every holiday, every marriage, every birth, was a bittersweet happening. We felt blessed by the joy but hurt by my father's absence. "If only he were here to see this," was the common refrain. But as time has passed, I have begun to feel his presence at moments of joy and it has made those moments more joyous.

There is an ancient Jewish belief that the souls of deceased parents are present when their children get married. Because of this belief, it is a custom to invite deceased parents to the wedding. After all, if the dead are going to come to the wedding anyway, why make them crash the party?

About a month before our wedding, Rob and I took a special trip back to New York. One day we rented a car and drove from rush-hour-packed Manhattan out to New Jersey, past the sprawling suburban homes, until we reached the eternal homes of my ancestors. The cemetery looked like an orchard of tombstones, and we spent close to an hour just trying to find the right location.

Then we reached my father's stone. It had these words from the Psalms written on it: "He who lives with integrity, does what is right, and speaks the truth in his heart." Then it listed my father's name, the dates of his birth and death, followed by "Superb husband, beloved father and brother." It's so difficult to sum up a life in just a few words. But what else belongs on an epitaph? Ultimately, I suppose, our relationships are our greatest accomplishments. We spend so much time in this life worrying about success, but our greatest successes are the bonds we build. I've never seen a tombstone that read, "Great Accountant," or "Made Millions," or "Vice President of Sales," or "Drove a Porsche."

We stood before my father's grave in silence. Then I gathered up all my courage and said, "Hi, Daddy, this is Rob. I love him. I'm sure that you're going to love him too. We're getting married on April 14 and we'd like to invite you to the wedding. We hope you can come."

On the morning of the fourteenth, I was a bundle of nerves. My mother helped me get dressed in my white bridal gown, then I headed off to my synagogue. The entire congregation had come to share in our joy, and the sanctuary was packed to overflowing. I held my mother's hand as we prepared for the long march down the aisle toward the wedding canopy. As we walked arm in arm, I felt blessed with love—on *both* sides. I knew that my father was there with me. He had come to give the bride away.

On the day of my son's bris, as we brought our newborn baby into the room, a congregant of mine named Dorit turned to me and said, "Your father was here today." I replied, "I know."

Just two days before I write these words, my sister gave birth to a baby girl. When I spoke to her on the phone, she said that she wished our father could have been there to behold his granddaughter. I said to her, "He's there. I know he's there." She said, "I know too. I talk to him all the time."

Feeling his spiritual presence eases the hurt, but it doesn't erase it. I still long for my father's tangible presence. I long for my children to meet him, to know him, and to love him.

We all miss someone we have loved and lost. We are angry, we are crushed, we are lonely without them. And we always find ourselves asking *why*: Why did this happen? How could it have happened to such a good person? How could God have *let* it happen? I wish I could provide the answers to these questions. But no one can. There *are* no answers. Only questions. And it is our task to go on living with our questions, to strive for the best in ourselves despite our confusion, to accept that this world that God has created is filled with mysteries beyond our comprehension.

IN THE SIXTEENTH CENTURY, the city of Safed in northern Israel was home to the greatest mystical teachers of the Kabbalah, of Jewish mysticism. These great scholars preserved for us the Jewish mystical beliefs in reincarnation and the immortality of the soul. Students of the rational discarded these beliefs as utter nonsense. Elsewhere in the Land of Israel, the rabbis spent their days in legal debates and Talmudic argumentation; in Safed, answers to great questions could be found not only in the pages of the text but from the very mouth of God, from the mysterious world of the spirit.

In Safed the rabbis sought to bridge the gap between heaven and earth, between the living and the dead. Just imagine what the Sabbath must have been like! On Friday morning the great mystics would awaken and immerse themselves in the mikvah, in waters of purification. Then, after their morning prayers, they would begin the holy preparations for the Sabbath. The smells of sumptuous meals would waft through the streets as women made their homes and their children ready to receive the Sabbath Queen. At sunset, as the Sabbath drew near, the mystics would dress in white. They would light Sabbath candles, then gather outdoors in a field. There they would face west to welcome the Sabbath bride.

To these mystics the Sabbath was not just a sacred time or a day of rest. To them the Sabbath was a presence, a spirit that was so palpable you could almost touch her. To them the Sabbath had a soul so real that if you stood beside her you would find yourself illuminated through her radiance. Their prayers grew ever more fervent as they searched for God's presence, as they yearned for signs of connectedness with souls who no longer walked the earth. The hunger within them was not a longing for bread or water but for God, a thirst for understanding God's ways, for hearing God's word. And as they stood in the darkening field, shoulder to shoulder, a sea of white robes fluttering as they swayed, they looked like God's ministering angels floating upward toward the throne of glory. A feeling of lightness overcame them, filling them with a hope that redemption was near, that this often cruel and painful world would at last be released from its misery and suffering. As the night descended upon them, their souls soared to such heights of holiness that they could hardly feel their feet touching the ground as they returned to their homes.

When my husband and I were in Israel, we visited Safed. As we made our way through the narrow cobblestone streets, we came upon the synagogue of the great mystic Rabbi Isaac Luria. The synagogue was built on the site of the field where the mystics used to gather to welcome the Sabbath. As I stood there, I couldn't help feeling that I was surrounded by the sacred souls of the ancient mystics. And as we each sit in our homes right now, I wonder if we are sitting in the presence of souls we cannot see.

At Isaac Luria's synagogue in Safed, there is a chair for Elijah which is left empty in the hope that the spirit of Elijah the Prophet will visit us and save us. My own belief is that wherever life takes us, there are always going to be empty seats. Not just for Elijah but for all those we mourn. I believe that we are surrounded by the presence of those we have loved and lost. And I pray that their presence will continue to be with us, to influence our lives for the better in death as they did so beautifully in life.

CHAPTER THIRTY-ONE

Our Broken Pieces

NO MATTER HOW HARD WE TRY to recover from a hurt, no matter how much time has passed, there will always be pieces of ourselves that will remain broken. We may search for ways to erase all traces of our painful past, but we will never succeed. Our wounds may heal, but the scars that are left behind are indelible. They will be with us, in some form, for the rest of our days on this earth. The scars may not be visible the way that battle scars are, but they are just as real. Sometimes I wish that emotional scars could be seen. At least that way it would prevent us from denying them.

I will always be a woman whose father was murdered when she was a girl. Yes, I have learned to make peace with certain aspects of my loss, I continue to learn new ways to grow and heal, I have even become stronger and wiser as a result of this tragedy, but ultimately the scar that's left from that loss will be with me forever.

I miss my father every day and I will never *not* miss him. I want to ask him questions that he will never answer. I want to feel his reassuring hand on my head. I want to smell his smell again. But I never will. And it hurts. It will *always* hurt.

Over time, some things hurt less. The void that my father's absence left in my life has been partially filled by new joys, by my husband, by my son and my daughter.

But with the passage of time some things hurt more. I wish my husband could have known my father. I wish that my children could have loved their grandfather. As time passes, I feel as if I know less and less about my father. I have trouble conjuring up his image in my mind. Nothing will ever take away that hurt. I will always be trying to make sense of my father's death.

Michelle has come a long way since the day she was raped. She's married, with a son, a home, a community, a new life. "Time does heal," she told me. "I was sure my life was over, but now I see that *good* things happen to good people, too." And yet, even though she has embraced so many of those good things, the scars remain. Her nose is still slightly crooked from where the rapist struck her. I can't see the difference, but she is acutely aware of it whenever she looks in the mirror. It reminds her of the horror, and of the fact that she is forever changed. Whenever anyone, even her husband, walks up behind her unexpectedly, she jumps in fear or freezes in panic. Once she was visiting a friend who had to change her baby's diaper in a parking lot. This friend laid her child in the trunk of her car and proceeded to diaper him. Michelle started to tremble and had to walk away. She told me that her next car won't have a trunk at all. She still has difficulty getting dressed up; she always prefers pants to a skirt and feels uncomfortable making herself look attractive.

Simply going outside alone continues to be a struggle for Michelle. When she took her son for his four-month checkup, the doctor told her, "My prescription is that it's time to take the baby out for a walk." The very next day she gently placed her child in the stroller and walked him all the way to the dry cleaner's and back. She did it all by herself, and it was a major breakthrough. The next day she did it again. Taking her child out for a walk is no longer a mountain to climb, but it is still a challenge. And it may *always* be a challenge.

Keith will always have to contend with his gambling addiction. His paycheck goes directly into a bank account that he cannot touch.

Sam told me that because of his Holocaust experiences, he has a permanent emotional scar that will never go away. When something horrible happens, he has no reaction. Sometimes people think he is being callous or insensitive. But he can't control it. He just can't seem to get worked up about anything— even moments of joy. He may be happy, but he can never get *too* happy. His emotions just aren't all there. He also has trouble making deep connections with people. As Sam puts it, "I've never had real enemies. Real friends, either."

Molly always fears that whenever people leave, it might be the last goodbye. She remembers only too well how her father left for a weekend and never returned. She now hates it when people walk out the door without offering a hug, a kiss, or some expression of their love. When someone merely waves goodbye, it truly frightens her. She always needs to say a *real* goodbye. Even to her two dogs. She always has to hug and kiss them when she comes and goes.

Louis, who barely survived the Holocaust, still suffers from occasional bouts of depression. These are periods when he is plagued by persistent flashbacks, when he takes no pleasure in life. Not even in the sight of his beautiful grandchildren.

Whenever Mike has financial pressures, whenever he is fatigued, he is tempted to drink again. He still has to do daily battle with the side of him that longs to escape from all pain and sadness. He now understands that there *is* no real escape. He must learn to live with his pain, to face it head-on.

Dennis and Kathy will continue to miss their daughter Rebecca every day of their lives for as long as they live. My mother will always be a woman who watched the man she loved so much get shot.

. . .

WHAT ARE we to do with the broken pieces of ourselves? All too often we try to ignore them, deny them, or obliterate them, never realizing that they will be with us for the rest of our days on this earth. We try to bury our shattered parts because we see them as a sign of weakness, as a painful reminder of our vulnerability. But our broken pieces are a seat of wisdom and insight and compassion within us. They are holy and sacred and ought to be preserved.

What did Moses do with the broken tablets? The ones he threw to the ground when he saw the Children of Israel worshipping the golden calf. What could he possibly have done with those shards of stone? They were useless, unreadable. They were in pieces.

Moses went back up the mountain to carve out a new set of tablets and to receive the words of the Ten Commandments once more. He came down from the mountain with this replacement set of unbroken, freshly hewn tablets of stone, and he presented them to the Children of Israel, who built a holy ark, the Ark of the Covenant, to house them. The Israelites carried the ark with them throughout all their journeys in the desert. They brought it with them into the Promised Land, and eventually placed it inside the holy Temple that King Solomon built.

But what became of the broken pieces?

Legend has it that inside the Ark stood the tablets of the Ten Commandments, and right beside them there rested the *broken* tablets which Moses had shattered on that fateful day.

Moses understood that the broken tablets could not just be discarded or ignored. He saw that, even though they were broken and illegible, they were holy because they came from God. They were holy precisely *because* they were in pieces. They were an important reminder of an awful experience of idolatry and betrayal which he prayed would never be forgotten. *Should* not be forgotten. The teaching they imparted was just as powerful as the teaching of the Ten Commandments themselves.

. . .

WHEN I FIRST became a rabbi, people would ask me, "How are you going to be able to help people through tragedies when you're so young? What do you know about pain?" And I would laugh to myself. I was only twenty-six, but I felt like I had taken a crash course in life experience. I never doubted for one minute that I would be able to help people who were suffering. My painful experiences have shaped the person I have become. Without them I probably would never have wrestled with my religion, with God. I probably would never have become a rabbi. I am sure I would have been a lot more carefree, a lot less dark, and less angry. Certainly a lot less wise and a lot less empathetic. I probably would never have known my own strength.

Jane is the daughter of Dorothy and David, the couple whose home was destroyed in the fire, and she is also a dear friend of mine. Jane told me that often her mom would take out an heirloom and say, "This was Grandma's, and when I'm gone this will be yours." And Jane was so moved to know that she was in the line of transmission of a precious legacy. Whenever she looked at a dish or a tray that had belonged to her great-grandmother, she thought, "One day this will be mine." But now the chain of tradition is broken. Misty-eyed, Jane told me that somehow it's easier to feel closer to departed loved ones when you are sipping from a cup that their lips once touched, when you're wearing a wedding ring that they wore for fifty years, or when you're staring at a photograph of their face. In some ways, losing those items was like losing the dead all over again. Now there is no remnant of their presence left to hold on to. Jane said, "Now I feel an enormous responsibility to remember in a new way, to keep the memory of my grandparents and great-grandparents alive without any visual aids or props. It's like Judaism always says—we have to smash our idols and believe in all the things we can't see. Because that's all that really matters in the end. It's the love, the tenderness, the humor, and the wisdom that truly survive." Jane also told me that it is only in a crisis that you really get to see who people are. And to see her parents respond to this loss with such dignity and grace, with such hope and determination to carry on, makes her honored to be their child. "That is the invaluable lesson they have given me," Jane explained. "That is my inheritance, and nothing can ever take *that* away."

Sometimes we forget this simple truth: The broken pieces of ourselves are often our greatest teachers. It is from them that we learn our strength. It is from them that we learn compassion, wisdom and understanding, devotion, faith, and insight. It is from them that we learn how to pray, how to cry, how to listen, how to reach out for help. It is from them that we learn how to strive for better, how to empathize and offer help.

A Prayer

My wounds may heal, God, but my scars may never fade. Help me to embrace them, not despise them. Teach me how to live with my broken pieces, how to tend to them, how to learn from them. Remind me that I possess the power to turn my curses into blessings, my shame into pride, my sadness into strength, my pain into compassion.
Amen.

CHAPTER THIRTY-TWO

A Sacred Scroll

JUST BECAUSE there are broken pieces inside us does not mean that *all* of us is broken. Having scars does not mean that we are damaged goods, irredeemable or permanently tainted. Sometimes people feel so scarred by a hurt that they have trouble seeing the larger part of themselves that is left whole, perfect, and intact, the part that can *never* be broken or destroyed no matter what pains we have endured. I will never be the same person as I was before my father's murder. I've changed. Sometimes I try to remember what that Naomi was like. The one who was not hurt by life. But then I realize that there are parts of me that have not changed at all. There is an aspect of my being that doesn't need any healing because it can never be injured or ruined, it remains and will remain constant and firm.

When I was about twelve or so, I wanted to learn how to read from the Torah. All the boys in my class were studying Torah cantillation in preparation for their bar mitzvah ceremonies, but girls weren't permitted to join the class. I begged, pleaded, and protested, but the rabbi of my youth said, "When a girl gets her period, she's impure. If you touch the Torah when you're impure, you'll make the Torah impure." And that was the end of our discussion. In short, I should have known better than to want to contaminate the Torah.

It was years later, during my rabbinic training, that I learned that the rabbi of my childhood was wrong. It's true that Judaism views menstruation as a time of impurity. But the Torah can *never* receive that impurity. It is deemed so sacred by our tradition that *nothing* can render it impure. Nothing. Not even me.

Not even the most terrible and deliberate act of desecration can render a Torah impure. There is a horrifying account in rabbinic literature about how Titus defiled the Torah and the Temple. The narrative of that event reads just like a rape scene: "The wicked Titus entered the Holy of Holies with his sword drawn. He slashed the curtain and his sword came out covered with blood. . . . He took two prostitutes, spread out a Torah scroll beneath them, and proceeded to have sex with them on top of the altar."

Nothing has dominion over the holiness of a Torah scroll, not even its physical destruction. During the Roman persecutions in Israel, a great rabbi named Hanina ben Teradion was sentenced to death for openly teaching Torah in defiance of the Roman ban. The Talmud offers this account of his execution: "They took him, wrapped him in a Torah scroll, tied vines around him, and set them on fire. They took woolen sponges soaked in water and placed them over his heart, to make sure that he would not die too quickly. . . . His disciples cried, 'Master, what do you see?' He replied, 'The parchment is burning, but the letters are soaring up to heaven.'"

WITHIN EACH OF US, I believe, there lies a space that is as indestructible as a sacred scroll. A space that is holy and eternal, unalterable and untarnishable. A space of purity and wisdom. It is this space that enables us to find the strength to rebuild our lives after tragedy. Not even death can have dominion over it. When we die, it soars upward back to God just like the letters of the Torah. Call it the soul, the life breath, the spirit. We all have access to it. It is the seat of God within each of us. Not the God of my childhood fantasies who comes to our rescue like Superman. Not the God who can prevent evil or cure disease. But the God who can heal us by being beside us in our suffering. The God who gives us strength to dream once more. The God who assures each and every one of us, *You are not alone, I am with you.*

A PRAYER

When I feel tainted, God, remind me that I am holy. When I feel weak, teach me that I am strong. When I am shattered, assure me that I can heal. When I am weary, renew my spirit. When I am lost, show me that You are near.

Amen.

CHAPTER THIRTY-THREE

What Good Is God?

WHAT GOOD is God? This is the question that Michelle asked me some seven years ago, and this is the question most of us face when we have endured a blow. Isn't God supposed to help me? Why did God let this happen to me?

Once I was teaching a Bible class and a very astute lawyer asked to speak to me after class. He said he could understand why the Jews in biblical times believed in God. They *experienced* God. They knew how God helped them. They heard God's voice uttering the words of the Ten Commandments. They had prophets who had close contact with God and who revealed God's will to them. They saw God's miracles with their own eyes—the ten plagues over Egypt, the parting of the Red Sea, the manna that fell from heaven. God led them through the desert with a pillar of cloud by day and a pillar of fire by night. But what this man wanted to know was how God helps us today. What happened to that obvious God of the Bible? Why doesn't God talk to us? Why doesn't God swoop down and save us? Where are our prophets? Where are our miracles?

I told him I believed that God has always been the same. It's human beings who have changed. Most of us no longer see an earthquake as a manifestation of divine fury. We no longer see a rainbow as a manifestation of a divine covenant. The Bible depicted God in anthropomorphic terms. It read natural occurrences as demonstrations of either divine salvation or divine punishment. I believe that God's presence has always been subtle, something we have to constantly search for. Of course, it's much harder to have a relationship with a God who is concealed, who doesn't always prevent horrible things from happening, than it is to believe in a God who is manifest in clear empirical ways. But that is our challenge.

Every so often, when I am performing a funeral, there is a family member of the deceased who looks at me with utter venom and says, "What do you have to say to this, Rabbi?" And I am reminded of Edward G. Robinson's character in *The Ten Commandments* who slyly complains, when the Children of Israel are in trouble, "Where's your God now, Moses?"

I wish I had the definitive response to the question of God and the existence of evil, but of course I don't. People often put this question to me as if it were my job to answer it. But I don't consider it my responsibility to defend God or apologize for God. People think that just because I am a rabbi, I must be God's press secretary. That's not the case. I am not engaged in some staged cover-up. I too get angry, frustrated, and confused.

But I do believe it is God who enables us to return to life after tragedy—not by eradicating all evil but by giving us the strength and the courage to face evil and to combat it. By giving us the capacity to appreciate the miracles that surround us each day, the conscience to choose good over evil, the compassion to extend our hands to those who are suffering.

Of course, there will always be times when we feel that God has disappeared from our lives. There will be times when we pray and feel nothing but our own longing for God. This feeling that God has vanished is as old as Judaism itself. In the Bible Job cries out: "Would that I knew how to reach God, how to get to God's dwelling place. . . . But if I go East—God is not there; West—I still do not perceive God."

There was a period of time in 1989 when I felt positively lost.

I was nervous about being the rabbi of a congregation. I was feeling overwhelmed by the hordes of people coming at me with so many needs and wants, expecting answers and solutions. My phone was ringing off the hook at home all night long, and, of course, every person felt that his or her particular problem was of ultimate importance. In a single night one congregant called in a panic to tell me that the synagogue newsletter had to go out the next day; he wanted me to open up the office and get a crew of volunteers to stamp them. Another called to tell me she had just had a breakthrough in therapy—she had recovered a lost memory of sexual abuse. A third congregant called to complain—at length—about one of the preschool teachers. I was drowning.

Then a woman named Sophie entered my life. Sophie had been the executive director of a major Los Angeles synagogue for decades, and she had seen it all. She came to my synagogue to teach me and my board how to get organized. She must have been in her mid-sixties, but she looked like someone in her eighties. She had sparse white hair, a voice that was deepened from too many cigarettes, and a complexion that was mottled from too much sun. Her skin hung loosely over her bones. The balding hair and the bass voice made Sophie seem androgynous. She spoke with the authority of a man but with the sensitivity of a woman.

The first thing Sophie taught me was that the rabbi sets the mood of the synagogue. If the rabbi is tense, the congregants will be tense. If the rabbi is calm, the congregants will feel calm. If I could maintain an air of composure, then those around me would start to feel less anxious as well. Sophie described to me how just that morning she had been sitting at an outdoor café when a stray German shepherd approached. The people sitting there started to panic. No one wanted to touch the dog. In a frenzy, the manager tried to shoo the dog away, which, of course, only made him bark. Sophie told the manager to bring her some string. She called the dog over, tied the string around his neck, then around the base of her chair and continued to sip her coffee in peace. "If people could only calm down a little," Sophie said, "they'd see how simple it is to handle whatever they are facing." Sophie told me that the most successful rabbi she had known was a man who spent all his time schmoozing with his congregants on the golf course. Everyone loved him, and he never worked too hard. He made everyone feel at ease.

Well, I knew that I wasn't going to be a hit on the golf course, but I did begin to see Sophie's point. I tried it and it worked. The calmer I was, the calmer those around me became.

The next time we met, Sophie taught me that people often label situations as absolute emergencies when they are not. "*Nothing* is an emergency," Sophie calmly explained. "Except a death."

Sophie said that some of the most successful people in the world are those who appear to have all the time in the world. There are people who always seem harried and in a rush, and they make everyone around them crazy. The special leaders, who may be busy beyond belief, *always* seem completely relaxed, as if they had plenty of time for everything they needed to do.

I decided to do my best not to let life's hectic pace get to me. People would charge into my office in a panic. I would respond to them in a slow and calm manner, and they would slow down, too. People would press me to make hasty decisions. I would take my time and turn an urgent situation into a peaceful discussion. My whole life started to change, and my entire congregation and staff started to change with me.

Then one day I got an urgent phone call. Sophie had collapsed in the hallway of my synagogue. I raced to the hospital, and I prayed as the doctors pounded on her chest. I stood there with my rabbi's manual reciting prayers as they injected her with drugs and defibrillated her. It was horrible seeing Sophie lying there on the table. I turned away at the sight of her naked-ness. To me she was this vibrant personality who just happened to be housed in that body; to the doctors and nurses she was just a body with a name.

A nurse rummaged through Sophie's purse to see if she was taking any prescription medications. To my surprise, she found a bottle of Valium. Suddenly that unflappable exterior of Sophie's seemed more human and vulnerable. Suddenly I understood how difficult it really is to remain calm in the face of life's ups and downs.

Hours later a doctor informed Sophie's husband that she was brain-dead.

After Sophie was transferred to a private room, her husband asked me to recite a prayer over her. As I began to pray over Sophie's comatose body, her pale blue eyes suddenly flung wide open. I must have jumped ten feet in the air. The nurse told me it was just a reflex, that Sophie couldn't possibly have known I was there, but I believe she did know. Several hours later she was pronounced dead.

Once again Sophie was right. The only real emergency is a death.

In the days after Sophie's death, I found myself roaming around almost in a daze. I wanted to feel comforted, but I couldn't *find* any comfort. I wanted to feel God's presence, but I couldn't find God anywhere.

I'm not exactly sure why Sophie's death hit me as hard as it did. My irrational side felt personally responsible for her death. She had been at the synagogue that day meeting with volun-teers from morning till night. If only she hadn't been working so hard, maybe she wouldn't have died. I also felt guilty because I had gone home for the night exhausted, while she had remained at the synagogue to address yet another meeting. Perhaps I should have urged her to leave. Perhaps I should have invited her to my home for dinner. Perhaps . . .

Another side of me was angry at God. How could a woman be allowed to die when she had been so feverishly engaged in the service of God? She was helping to save a synagogue; didn't she deserve a *little* extra divine attention?

Still another side of me recognized just how futile my prayers were as I watched Sophie's doctors fighting to stabilize her. I felt silly standing there in the ER with my rabbi's manual. I wanted to *do* something. I wanted to be able to save her, but all I could do was to feel helpless.

One morning I woke up and realized that I needed to go somewhere to find God again. I drove to a beautiful garden and I sat and prayed beside a pond. I felt strange praying so fervently to God when people were strolling by and staring at me, but something inside me propelled me forward. I fed the ducks, prayed some more, and I wept. But I didn't feel any better. I felt positively empty and alone. I watched a solitary white swan preening herself for over an hour, and I thought about how nice it must be to have no worries in the world, to just sit there in the water pecking at your white feathers all day. Nearby I noticed a man in a turban, deep in prayer. As I sat there, I thought about how different all the world's religions are and yet how similar are all our longings. No matter what our faith, we are all searching for signs of comfort from the same God. We are all praying and hoping to be heard.

Later that night I received my answer. It wasn't a voice and it wasn't a vision: it was an overwhelming feeling of *un*loneliness. For a brief moment I felt as close as I have ever felt to experiencing oneness. I could suddenly sense the connection between all things. I felt whole, full, warm, abundant. I felt God. And I broke down and cried in gratitude for that fleeting gift of insight.

God has given us life. And God is here to help us return to life when we have suffered. God has given us a heart, and God is here to help us feel once more. God has given us a soul, and God is here to help us soar once more. God has given us courage, and God is here to help us fight once more. God has given us hope, and God is here to help us dream once more. God has given us this very moment, and God is here to help us experience it in all its sacred glory.

IN THE YEARS since my father's death, my family has slowly returned to life. We have celebrated marriages, births, and holidays together. My mother has learned how to experience joy once more and how to live alone without feeling lonely.

In the years since my father's death, I have learned to trust, to hope, and to laugh again. After my first marriage, I somehow learned how to open my eyes, my heart, and my arms again. Throughout our lives we will, we should, feel the pain of our losses, the scars still present even after much time has passed. But we will also feel the strength of our spirit, the ability to persevere in the face of pain. The power to dream despite the many nightmares of existence. The stamina to push forward into the future carrying our past with us all the while. This is the power of God within us. This is our hope, our salvation. This is how we begin again.

A NOTE ABOUT THE AUTHOR

NAOMI LEVY was in the first class to admit women to study for the rabbinate at the Jewish Theological Seminary of America, and the first female Conservative rabbi to lead a congregation on the West Coast. She lives in Venice, California, with her husband, Robert Eshman, and their children, Adin and Noa.